THE MONSTER INSIDE OF ME

KATE L. WILHOIT

authorHOUSE

AuthorHouse™
1663 Liberty Drive
Bloomington, IN 47403
www.authorhouse.com
Phone: 1 (800) 839-8640

© 2017 Kate L. Wilhoit. All rights reserved.

No part of this book may be reproduced, stored in a retrieval system, or transmitted by any means without the written permission of the author.

Published by AuthorHouse 09/11/2017

ISBN: 978-1-5462-0777-1 (sc)
ISBN: 978-1-5462-0776-4 (e)

Print information available on the last page.

Any people depicted in stock imagery provided by Thinkstock are models, and such images are being used for illustrative purposes only. Certain stock imagery © Thinkstock.

This book is printed on acid-free paper.

Because of the dynamic nature of the Internet, any web addresses or links contained in this book may have changed since publication and may no longer be valid. The views expressed in this work are solely those of the author and do not necessarily reflect the views of the publisher, and the publisher hereby disclaims any responsibility for them.

Holy Bible, New International Version®, NIV® Copyright ©1973, 1978, 1984, 2011 by Biblica, Inc.® Used by permission. All rights reserved worldwide.

Contents

Prologue ix
Chapter 1 1
Chapter 2 5
Chapter 3 10
Chapter 4 13
Chapter 5 15
Chapter 6 18
Chapter 7 21
Chapter 8 23
Chapter 9 25
Chapter 10 27
Chapter 11 30
Chapter 12 35
Chapter 13 39
Chapter 14 42
Chapter 15 45
Chapter 16 48
Chapter 17 51
Chapter 18 54
Chapter 19 56
Chapter 20 60

Chapter 21 63
Chapter 22 66
Chapter 23 71
Chapter 24 75
Chapter 25 79
Chapter 26 82
Chapter 27 83
Chapter 28 86
Chapter 29 89
Chapter 30 95
Chapter 31 102
Chapter 32 109

Epilogue..113

This book is based on actual events throughout my life. I must warn you, my story is not for the squeamish. So, if you are easily offended, I urge you to put this book down. I wrote this book using journals I have kept over the years, and it is TRUTH....so brace yourselves, it's going to be a bumpy ride...

"He who fights with monsters might take care lest he thereby become a monster. And if you gaze for long into an abyss, the abyss gazes also into you." Friedrich Nietzsche.

Prologue

Joseph Conrad said, "The belief in a supernatural source of evil is not necessary. Men alone are quite capable of every wickedness..."

"Pop! Pop! Pop!" that noise that's been in my head for years. Now, every day, that specific sound, and the visions of my memories, haunt my soul. Then it finally dawned on me, that monsters aren't born, we are created. "Pop! Pop! Pop! I can smell it, a smell that would make me vomit to this day…liquor and blood. It's a sweet smell, that if you've EVER smelled, you will NEVER forget! "Pop! Pop! Pop! The screams ring through my ears. "OMG! You're pushing my face in!" a quote I will Never forget. I put my baby sister in our room, return to the living and scream at the top of my lungs "OMG! You're killing her Daddy! Please, please, please, Don't kill my Mommy!" I still struggle to get that image out of my head! "Gee! Gee! Gee-Ya!" he growls. Now, he is kicking my mother in the face. The sound of the connection of his foot to my Mother's face is indescribable, it's a solid thump, that you know with every connection, she's going to look less and less like your mommy, and more and more like a living nightmare.

I disconnect, drift off into thought, physically frozen. Presently, the thought is crossing my mind. "Was the final blow that smashed my Mother's beautiful teeth out of her face honestly from her falling?" Possibly, she was a serious black out alcoholic. More likely than not however, it was from years of face bashing at the hands of her father, and then at the hands of mine. My father frequently loosened her teeth, and my sister and I were instructed NEVER to discuss these horrible, scary, events with anyone. I remember being in the first grade and looking around my classroom and wondering to myself, "I wonder how many other Daddy's hit other Mommy's? Was I only one with this big secret? Did other kids have tummy aches that twisted their tummies into knots at the thought of leaving their Mommy's home with their Daddies, while we tried to get through a school day. First grade is scary. It's too long to be away from Mommy! I can't breathe the walls are closing in! My stomach hurts so bad I want to scream! But I can't, because than they would know! Did other kids have a suitcase packed and ready to go for the next time we get pulled out of bed in the middle of the night to run away from my Daddy?

I don't want to leave Daddy! He is screaming and crying on his knees! He is saying he is sorry. I sometimes slap my sissy when I'm mad, am I like Daddy? I never said a word… to ANYBODY! Grandma Well always said "Dana Leigh, these things happen in families, but we don't go around talking about it. All your Mommy and Daddy have to do is put down the booze, and everything will be fine, but they have to do it in their own time. If you talk to anybody about these things, they will come into your home, and take you and your sissy to foster care. Meaning you two girls will be separated and go live with other families, and you may never see each other again. You have to be strong Dana Leigh, you have to protect your baby sister! You two are all each of you have in this entire world, and as of this moment, it's your responsibility to protect your baby sissy, you can do this, I believe in you!" My mother's face was healing. Her face was colorful through a majority of my childhood. Her face was looking so much better, "maybe Daddy is serious this time, maybe he'll never hurt Mommy again." So, now nothing, silence for a few months, but the question that ran through my young mind was "Which haunted me more? The quiet? Or the sound of my Daddy squeezing the life out of my Mommy's face until I could see those spots? I hate those spots! Mommy lied to her my Grandma Well (her Mommy) and told her she came in contact with strawberries. Is she even allergic to strawberries? I knew better, but I let my baby sister believe the lies for her own protection.

Mommy could not cover her smell, that awful smell… blood and booze! My mommy gets spots all over her face and gets that smell after Daddy chokes her. I was six years old, and already had enough rage in my heart that I knew one day I was personally going to kill my Daddy. I was going to do it myself, nobody else, because he was my Daddy, and nobody was going to hurt him! That was for me to do. I had visions of bashing his head in, then changing his clothes, after cleaning him up, and kissing his cheek. I had a lot on my plate! And now my tummy was on fire again! Stupid tummy!" Mommy lies to Grandma Well so much, I think she believes them herself! Pop! Pop! Pop! His fists connecting with her face always made that same sound. Why won't this stop? I'm so tired, maybe I'm having a heart attack? Can you have a heart attack in the first grade?

My Father controlled my Mother's every move. He controlled her completely. My Father curled my Mother's hair and applied her make up. Blue eyeshadow, it would blend in with her black eyes he had recently given her. I'm sorry I hit you! It will never hit you again! The first lie I recall my Daddy ever telling. Mommy tried to leave so many times…off to the battered women's shelter we went, everyone knew us there! It was so fun for sissy and I, we met other kids who had mean daddies. So, it's not just mine? Like clockwork however, every time Mommy was set up to live with just us girls, something in Daddy's voice would draw her back. The crying, the explanations, the love they had that EVERYONE was trying to keep her from. Nobody understood he hit her because he loved her so much, he just gets out of control sometimes, but he'll try this time and NO MORE ALCOHOL.

I did not yet understand the connection, didn't really understand what alcohol was. But I would soon learn. I never asked my Mommy, "Why does Daddy hit you? I was so ashamed I couldn't even mutter the words to my own mother, what a shame, huh? I couldn't ask Mommy, I couldn't ask Anybody! I was screaming inside and nobody could hear me! Please throw my sissy and I a line, we need help! However, nobody could hear my cries, just my tummy, and it really hurts!" Every time Daddy beat Mommy, it was worse and lasted longer, sometimes Daddy would take breaks. But there were times these beatings would last a couple days, and boy were they long days! It's hard for me to take care of sissy and cover mommy so Daddy will stop hitting her, after all, I'm only six! I'm more scared of the quiet than I am the dark, because if it was quiet, I knew it, Mommy is finally dead, he finally killed her this time. However, the sounds of her gurgles, and choking, and cries became a comfort. If mommy was gurgling, she was fighting to live, and she WAS alive.

I want to stab Daddy, pull him off of her, but I can't, I'm too little, I'm only six. But one day, I'm going to grow up, and I'm going to bash HIS face! I'm going to choke him and grind his face into the couch, and grind my knuckles into HIS ribs until he screams! I love my Daddy, but one day I'm going to be a grown up, and I'm going to protect my mommy, and I'm going to beat my daddy like a dog!!! I'm going to always protect my mother and my sissy. Nobody can hit my Daddy though, nobody can hit anyone I love in my life ever again, because I will be a grown up, and I will smash their face and beat them until they are dead!" Now all I can do right now while Daddy is beating Mommy is concentrate on her life… take all my feelings and give them to her! "Play Dead Mama! And then he'll quit hitting you, and you will live to see another day with sissy and I.

Chapter 1

"Eldred Street and the Night that I Died"

"There are certain clues at a crime scene, which, by their very nature do not lend themselves to being collected or examined. How does one collect love, rage, hatred, and fear...?"

-James Reese

I have NEVER forgot that night. Daddy talked Mommy into coming home with us girls. Then they opened it that pretty bottle that when Mommy and Daddy drink it, they get crazy. I hate that bottle, it turns Daddy into a Demon. It's something called Vodka. I put my baby sister to bed and packed our suitcase, I could feel it in my little bones, we were in for a long night. I wasn't six anymore, I was eight, I was a big girl, and there was a storm coming, and I was ready. I was going to protect my sissy, she didn't deserve this, she had just started kindergarten, and she wasn't like me, she was a leader. My sissy's tummy didn't hurt when she was in school, she didn't worry about Mommy she was just a baby, and I didn't want her to ever feel mean like me. Sometimes when Mommy and Daddy were sleeping, I would stand at the foot of their bed thinking about stabbing my Daddy, and boy oh, boy did my stomach burn. But now it's time to focus, I don't want to see my sissy cry. Here it came again the silence, so I kissed my sissy's cheek and went downstairs and saw something that I will NEVER forget.

My parent's completely naked, Daddy choking Mommy, his hands are squeezing her throat so hard her eyes are starting to pop out of her face! All I could hear was that awful gurgling sound. I reached for the phone to call the police, but they were ripped out of the wall, it was all too real this time, that pretty angel with the black wings that talks to me in my room sometimes is going to take my mom to that place she tells me about. She is going to take my Mommy to that beautiful place that she will no longer feel any pain. That pretty angel plays with my hair sometimes when I'm too scared to sleep, she is really pretty, and she wants to take me away, but I don't want to leave my family here, not even my Daddy, because he is good inside, he'll show everyone someday. Go away pretty angel, come back another time.

Back to reality, my Daddy was choking Mommy while they were having sex. Why was he doing this? Why was he hurting her? If this is what sex is, if this is what boys grow up to be, I never want to get married. This was an unusually long night, now my Daddy starting kicking Mommy in the head, and the first time I saw him stomp on her, I ran out the front door. I ran outside in my nightgown with no shoes or socks and the snow was almost up to my waist. I had to get the neighbor James. He would save my Mommy, I just hope I can get him in time! My legs were burning and now my feet are numb. It doesn't hurt anymore, I can't feel anything. Is that pretty black angel helping me? When she gets too close to my face it feels like she is taking my breath away, but not now, I have a job to do, save my Mommy. James answered his door and I told him my Dad was trying to kill my Mom, he put his coat on, wrapped me in a blanket, and carried me home. He pulled my Dad off my Mom and they all sat down at the dining room table. But then they ALL started drinking that Vodka stuff, and they got loud, as well as the music. I quickly figured this night was only going get worse, and I think I poured gasoline on the grill. After this, my memory fades, however sometime later in the night, Dad returns to beating Mom. By this time y sissy and I were both watching. We were holding hands then dad just started beating mom over and over with his fist balled up all over the head and face, there was blood everywhere. Then one of my worst memories were created, I watched my baby sister screaming so hard her little veins were bulging out of her little baby neck, crocodile tears shot out of her huge brown eyes and she started pulling fists of her own hair out. I don't recall how long this went on, but my Mommy eventually broke free and stabbed my dad between his ribs with a dinner fork. Then he hit my Mommy so hard I remember she hit, flat on her back on the floor.

Then my Daddy delivered the final blow. I'll never forget, he grabbed her by her hair, and hit her so hard, he knocked her lights out literally. Her face literally instantly broke, and that's when I realized my worst fear came true! He finally did it…he "Pushed her face in!" The police busted through the back door, and there was my mom on the kitchen floor!

He did it! He finally killed my Mommy, and that was the day I died inside! Mommy looked so scary to me her face was completely mangled. Why did she do this? Why did she fight back? Why didn't she play dead? That was the night my mommy died and crazy Tam-Rock was born. I don't recall my conversation with the dispatch operator, Hell, I called the police so many times, I couldn't keep them separated. Mommy left on a stretcher and the police were very mean to my Daddy, they slammed him around, handcuffed him and took him to jail with no shoes, shirt, or coat in the bad snowstorm. Off to Grandma Well's house sissy and I went. A couple weeks went by, and Daddy took us to see Mommy in the hospital, but sissy and I were too scared to touch her, she looked like a Monster!

Chapter 2

"Daddy"

French poet Jacques Rigaut said, "Don't forget that I cannot see myself, that my role is limited to being the one who looks in the mirror."

My father, Jack Wilhoit Jr., was born August 2, 1960. My father was born to a father who was 54 years older than him. My grandfather was a low functioning illiterate, who worked miracles as a carpenter, however could not read or write past the signature of his own name. He was a recovering alcoholic, twenty years before my father was born, my grandfather woke up from a black out drunk, smashed his whiskey bottle in the river, and decided to never put that poison back in his body...and he DIDN'T. My grandfather was the direct product of incest between his mother and her father, and spent a majority of his childhood locked away, hidden, he was the family secret. My grandfather left home as a teenager and served in the military, the details are very vague, but as a child, I did stumble upon his dog tags.

My grandfather was married once before my grandmother, and together they had a son...my "Uncle Sammy." My grandfather doted over his wife, for he loved her very much. One rainy afternoon however, tragic struck, and Sammy's mother dropped dead in front of my grandfather as they entered a department store. My grandfather learned she had blood clots in her head that ruptured. Later in life, my grandfather met my grandmother and they had two children, my father, Jack Wilhoit Jr. And my aunt "Leddie Ann Wilhoit." My grandfather was much older than my grandmother, and though I had never seen proof, it was rumored my grandfather had three official birth certificates, one as far back as 1909. To this day, I have no idea exactly how old my grandfather lived to be. He worked very hard to provide for my father's family, I'm assuming the best way he knew how.

My grandmother developed a serious alcohol problem. She never took a drink until the age of 45, and she managed to drink herself to death by the age of 54. During this time, she began to abuse my grandfather, who was a little man standing only 5'1. Given her German heritage, she was quite a bit larger than him and she used this to her advantage. She would fly into rages. My grandfather would cook her meals, even cutting her steak so she could chew it better. My grandfather treated my grandmother like a queen of the castle. However, he took his rage and anger out on his children, molesting his daughter, beating his son, and just all around being emotionally unavailable. When my father was 16, My grandfather forced my father to drop out of high school and go to work at the local laundry with my grandmother. He told my father that school was for "rich republicans and queers." My father suffered years of abuse from his father. He escaped into a world of music, taking guitar lessons. He was diagnosed with "Hyperactivity" and prescribed medications that would leave him in a zombie like state. You see before this medication, my father was so hyper that he would "Go" all day, and when he finally crashed at night, he would sleep so hard, he would urinate the bed.

The cure for this in my grandfather's eyes? Hang his sheets off the front porch for the neighborhood to see, and send my father to school in his soiled pajamas. I believe my grandfather thought he was just giving tough love, but what he didn't realize, was that he was breaking a very talented, very sweet boy's spirits.

After years of abuse from his father, my father experienced one of the most brutal examples of child abuse I have ever heard of. When he was twelve years old, his Uncle "Jimmy" entered his bedroom late at night and stole my father's childhood...Uncle Jimmy, was already feared by the children in the family, for he had a hook for his right hand (it was rumored he misfired, and blew it off in a drunken rage) late one night, he snuck into my father's room, put the hook to the back of his neck, and violated my father in the worst way imaginable. He tormented my father following this night, intimidating him, whispering in his ear, calling my father a "Queer" and a "Fairy." he gave my father an entire plate of chocolate to eat in front of my grandmother, which later in the evening sent my father to the emergency room. For these were NOT regular chocolates they were laxatives. When my father could take no more, he went to his mother. My grandmother became unglued and told my father "There were places for lying little boys like him." My father understood her completely, he understood, he was alone, and would just to have to endure this abuse until he was old enough to run.

My grandfather eventually died of lung cancer, but not before my grandmother broke his heart by leaving him for another man. My grandmother was a nurse at the VA hospital, and she had an affair with "Jamal", the head of the laundry. He was the complete opposite of my grandfather, he was a raging alcoholic. He was black, young, exciting, and full of adventure. He also loved my grandmother.

Jamal and my grandmother's relationship declined very fast, they began drinking every-day. Their alcohol intake quickly escalated from pints to 5ths to half gallons to cases, and it went from scotch to cheap rock gut vodka. My grandmother's alcoholism got so bad, she would "chase" her vodka shots with buttermilk to coat her stomach so she could even hold it down. My grandmother and Jamal would go on week long binges. Missing work and beating on each other. My father was called repeatedly to break them up. Later in life, Jamal would beat my grandmother with a glass "Coca-Cola" bottle in the head, until he passed out. This assault led my grandmother to having her head shaved and drilled to relieve the pressure from her brain, She was never the same after this. After this specific assault on my grandmother, my father and some buddies kicked Jamal's door in. My father kicked the telephone off the wall, and beat Jamal almost to death. My grandmother later died of a combination of liver failure and the injuries from the beating. My father watched his mother be lowered into the ground, but could not bring himself to cry. The pain was unbearable. My father was now officially an orphan, and all alone in the world.

Chapter 3

"Mommy"

"Birds sing after a storm; why shouldn't people feel as free to delight in whatever sunlight remains to them?"

-Rose Kennedy

My mom, Sandra (Well) Wilhoit, was born July 7, 1960. My mother was the youngest of seven children. My grandparents had a very unique relationship. My grandfather was a security guard, and my grandmother, a homemaker and part time Home Health Aide. They were married and raised their seven children together.

My grandfather, suffered from what was then known as "Manic Depression" or what we now refer to as Bipolar Disorder. My grandfather was a disturbed man, who often beat my grandmother, and was cruel to his children, mainly focusing on my mother, for she was the defiant one. My mother was the baby, and was very close to her mother. Due to this behavior my mother expressed, she often received severe beatings at the hands of her father. My grandfather once beat my mother from her butt, down the side of her leg with a cable chord. My mother was determined to protect her mother, which resulted in years of physical and emotional abuse. At one point, my grandfather tore my mother's birth certificate up in front of her face and told her she was trash, just like her mother. Shortly after this, my grandfather sat my mother in my grandmother's lap in a rocking chair, and punched my grandmother in the face, causing her and my mother to fly backwards to hit the floor. Before the end of their relationship, my grandfather had my grandmother committed to the sanitarium, where she was subject to brutal shock treatment therapy.

My grandfather later had an affair with the family's live in nanny, resulting in the birth of my mother's half- sister, my Aunt noel. My grandfather later left the nanny for yet, another woman, and later had my two youngest uncles. My mother witnessed years of domestic violence, was constantly moved from parent to parent, and eventually settled down with my grandmother.

Fast forward to the future, my grandmother met the love of her life, who I considered more of a grandpa than my actual one, a man who us grandkids would grow to know as Lenny G. Lenny was fun, and he was the king of practical jokes. Lenny and my grandmother had their share of up and downs, but Lenny was the total opposite of my grandfather. Lenny was fun, caring, and lighthearted, and he never abused my grandmother the way my grandfather did. Those were my grandparents, and at one time, my parents, and their deaths affected me hard. The death of my grandma worst so hard, I couldn't bring myself to attend her funeral.

One thing my grandmother and I had in common, neither of us believe in Heaven, we believe that when it's your time to go...that's it! Lights out! I gave up praying at a young age. God couldn't be real. If God was real, why would he expose my baby sister and I to such heartache? No matter how much I prayed throughout my trying times...he never showed up. Where was he when my grandfather went from the Daddy who let my mother stand on his feet while he danced with her, to the brutal son-of-a bitch that told her she was ugly, and would never be anything? What child deserves to live like that? For the rest of my mother's life, she had the most unbelievably low self-esteem, and would attract a man similar to her father.

Chapter 4

"The Ceilings"

"With foxes, we must play the fox..."

-Dr. Thomas Fuller

"The Ceilings." A local club/bar that was a very popular in the town of Indian Falls, Michigan. A town my parents were born and raised in as well as I would be. My parents both ended up there that night. My mother tells me they were both getting over bad break ups. My mother told me the night she met my father, he approached her, and whispered in her ear "Want to go get high?" She told me something inside of her told her to go. My parents smile when they tell me this story. Mom says she saw dad, his big curly locks, and puppy like brown eyes hooked her. My father says my mother was so tiny, so tan. He said she was wearing roman sandals, and a terry clothed sun dress, and she took his breath away.

Both of my parents were recovering from severe breakups, and neither of them wanted to be there that night. My mom was dragged out by her girlfriends, and my dad was trying to "shoot" his sorrows away, it was a special night at this club. This night was the one night a week, you could purchase a whole pitcher of mixed drinks for $1.75.

My mom went home with my dad that night, they partied, drank, enjoyed each other's company. They visited with friends, and my dad swept my mom off her feet with the most beautiful guitar music she had ever heard played. They then spent the first of what would be a lifetime of nights in bed together.

The next morning, my mother awoke to the smell of my dad cooking her breakfast. My mom said she was so nervous, she couldn't swallow a bite. She said she knew right then and there this was where she was supposed to be, right by his side. My mother moved in with my father the next day. Three months later, after what the doctors told my mother would be impossible, she became pregnant with me. To her surprise however, their lives were going to be far from a fairy tale, for soon she would be exposed to my father's jealous, violent rages. Through that however, my mother never thought twice about bringing a baby into the world.

Chapter 5

"Dana Leigh & Samantha Lynn"

"Other things may change us, but we start and end with family"

-Anthony Brandt

I never asked my mom for the details, I am well aware that her and dad fought while I was in the oven. My mother went into labor and 27 ½ hours later I was born. I was born on July 31, 1982. Then two years and nine months later, my baby sissy, Samantha Lynn was born on April 15, 1985. My mother almost lost her life bringing both, my sister and I into this world. The details are a bit foggy of the events that took place between my and my sister's births, and my mother doesn't like to discuss it, so I don't push the matter. What I DO know is that later in life, my mother informed my sissy just how excited my father was that I was coming into the world, and how disappointed he was that she was. "He never wanted you!" My mother told her, and that resulted in a permanent wedge between my father and my sister that still affects their relationship to this day.

Although I am only roughly three years older than my sister, I remember the day she came home from the hospital. My day started off crappy because I was stuck in the waiting room with one of my dad's band members who couldn't hold a note to save his life, lol! He decided to sing his rendition of Motley Crue's "Home Sweet Home" to me at an attempt to keep me occupied while my parents were packing up my baby sister.

I got in the back seat of the car, got all buckled in, got my juice box and was ready to roll, when all of the sudden, they put "THAT" in the backseat with me. What the hell was this? Nobody asked me if I wanted to bring this "thing" home with us. My stomach felt tight, my throat got all "gaggy", why couldn't we leave this at the hospital where it belongs? I was so hurt, so betrayed, so,so....PISSED! I was convinced if I put both feet on its car seat, I could surely knock it out of the car before we got home! I pushed and pushed, and cried. I felt like I was going to die!!! How could this be? I had to get rid of it!

When we got home, there were members of my family everywhere. My dad sat its car seat on the dining room table. Instantly, everybody wanted to get a peek at the new baby. What about "Dana Leigh?" Was everybody going to forget about me? I know, I'll run and grab my pom-poms and do a cheer...but nothing. I was scooted out of the way, nobody wanted to hear me, nobody wanted to watch me!

Finally, after what seemed like hours, they crowd broke up around my sister, I finally got my chance to peek at her. I didn't see what the big deal was, she looked like a wrinkled

Chapter 6

"A ticking time bomb, leading to my prologue...".

"Hiroshima Manufacturing"

Mexican Proverb..."The house does not rest upon the ground, but upon a woman."

I'm going to explain the events that led up to the nightmare of Eldred Street. A new car factory opened up in my home town of Indian Falls, Michigan. My father, having excellent automotive factory experience, applied for a job in this new factory. This was going to help change our lives. He was chosen out of 500 other applicants. My father had excellent test scor4es and was chosen as one of the "Original" Hiroshima Associates. My dad found his dream house, an upper and lower duplex apartment that had been opened up into one gigantic house! It was the biggest house I had ever seen! It was a wonderland to my baby sister and I, but would soon turn to a "House of Horrors!" Eldred street and dad's new job was going to change our family, it was going to save us.

THE MONSTER INSIDE OF ME

What my sissy and I were too young to understand, was that my mom was beginning to live in her own prison. My dad had over time, alienated her away from her friends and family, so all she had where us kids. My sissy and I where her friends. My mother tried to hide the drunken fights from us girls, with no success. My dad constantly reminded her that since she brought in no money, he made the rules. My father completely controlled her. My Mother's Day consisted of walking my sissy and I to school, then returning home to a loaded wine rack, full of expensive wine and good liquor... everything she was forbidden to touch! That is, until my father got out of work at night, and permitted my mother to drink with him.

My father was in complete control over every aspect of my mother's life...but that was soon about to change. How could my father light the fuse and expect it not to blow? My father didn't realize the pain and payback he was in for. All of those choke marks on my mother's face, all of those karate kicks to the face, all of those kidney shots and punches to the stomach, wasn't going to be able to light a candle to the pain my mother was about to inflict on him. All of the degrading things he did to her, his fits of rage, his unwritten rules, there was about to be a major shift in power. It was going to be like a tsunami crashing the shores. For the first time, HE was going to feel humiliated, stupid, ugly, insecure, not worth shit.... BROKEN. My father had a date with karma that my mother was going to make sure he wasn't late for.

My mother had supported my father's dreams over the years of being a professional musician. There were times my father was on the road more than he was home. He came home penniless, embarrasse4d, hopeless, and most of all ANGRY! My mother stayed by his side through everything, and how did he repay her? By turning my mother into an angry, resentful woman. While my dad was working at Hiroshima, my mother drank at least a gallon of wine a day, and this would ultimately lead her to meet "him." A man that my sissy and I grew to dislike more than our own dad, the one who was going to rip our family apart and forever change the dynamics that my sissy and I knew as our family.

Chapter 7

"The Demonic Leprechaun in the Red Truck"

"In a time of universal deceit, telling the truth is a revolutionary act"

-George Orwell

His name was Conner, and to be fair he didn't actually rip my family apart, but he was definitely the catalyst. Tired of being alone, underappreciated, beat on, degraded, yet expected to be a trophy wife, my mom reached out and started drinking with the neighbors. That is when she met him, and he had a bad reputation of sleeping with married women. My mother lived in a constant fog of intoxication, and she slowly began interacting with Conner. So right before Thanksgiving, the neighbors, mom, dad, and Connor all went to the hot tubs.

The more they all drank, the more my dad noticed a very intense environment between himself, my mother, and Conner. Now you'll have to forgive me, for I was only eight at this time, so the details of these events were through the eyes of a child. There are things I may have misunderstood, but this is my honest testimony as I recall it. It was now Thanksgiving, and dinner was put out on the table. Mom and dad had already been drinking. Mom couldn't handle the guilt anymore and she told my father what he already knew...She was having an affair with Conner. Then she swiped our entire Thanksgiving dinner off of the dining room table. Then while my dad proceeded to beat my mom, I assumed my usual role as Mama to my baby sister, saved what dinner I could off of the floor, and made a plate for my sissy. Happy Thanksgiving! Another fun filled holiday in the Wilhoit house.

Those were the events that led up to the worst night of my life on Eldred Street. When my mom was rushed to the hospital with a broken face, she was admitted for the third time in my life to the Adventist Hospital for a mandatory 30-day dry out. Her diagnosis was alcoholism/severe mental breakdown. As I got older, I learned the reason why my mother was so scary to me, the reason this last fight was so much different than the rest. She had said it exactly...my father HAD pushed her face in. That final blow he delivered to my mother's face, smashed the orbit of her eye. She had become the monster in my dreams. And I don't think I have ever recovered from that one.

Chapter 8

"The Ripple Effect"

"Of all animals, man is the only one that is cruel. He is the only one that inflicts pain for the pleasure of doing it"

-Mark Twain

My father had excellent insurance through his job at Hiroshima, which paid for my mother's treatment and allowed him to see a psychiatrist. This doctor prescribed my dad a fairly new medication that was being used for anxiety, known as xanax. My dad fell apart without my mom, and turned to liquor and xanax and began calling in to work. After he exhausted all of his allotted time off, his boss suggested he resign, and avoid the embarrassment of being taken before tribunal and being terminated. My dad dropped deep into a dark cloud of depression, lost weight, developed ulcers, and began to seclude himself from the world.

My father couldn't live with what he had done to my mother, or what she had done to him for that matter. He began to self-medicate, drinking in upwards of a half of a gallon of vodka per day. My dad later began to mix his liquor with his xanax producing the most animated black out drunk experiences. He had lost everything. He had lost his family. He lost the three girls that meant the most in his life, my mother and us girls. He was alone, just as he felt when his parents died and he became orphaned. What had he done? How could he make it better? He had hit rock bottom, if only he could have turned back time. He wouldn't have hurt my mom, he wouldn't have ignored her, he wouldn't have said those mean things to her. Is this how he made her feel? Surely death would be better than this feeling. No matter how much he drank, no matter how many pills he swallowed, no matter how many drugs he did, he would always wake up the next day. This was Hell, and he was Satan's tampon.

Things couldn't get much worse. If she would hear him out one final time, he would keep his promise this time. Things really would be different. He would never hit her again, he would be a better Daddy to his babies, and he would hold her tight and never let her go. What could he do to prove this? He couldn't handle the pain, he was dying, or at least he felt like he was. However, he wasn't getting out of it that easy....

Chapter 9

"Over the River and through the woods..."

Grandma Well lived two houses down from our elementary school. Grandma took temporary custody of sissy and I while mommy was in the Adventist Hospital. Dad was handling the stress of that, the loss of his good job, and barley holding on to his sanity. Grandma did the very best she could to take care of us. Grandma showed us lots of love, gave us a bedroom, cooked us breakfast, packed our lunch for school, and cooked us dinner every night. Grandma did her best to take care of us, although in my opinion, there is only one thing she did wrong...she told us stories about our father. These stories made me realize that my dad was NOT a monster, he was sick, and needed help. My grandma told me a story of my dad beating my mother unconscious with a dumbbell, and another story of him biting nearly biting her ear off.

And although I loved my grandmother very much, I needed that comfort of the very thing that I hated the most, I needed to hear those fights again. In my young, troubled mind, after seeing my dad he was always a monster. However now, for the first time, I felt like I understood my father. I wanted my family back. I needed that chaos to feel whole again... the very definition of sweet misery. I had promised myself that if what my parents had was love, I never wanted to experience that, not EVER. I would never put my children through the Hell, I went through. Nobody understood my family though, we needed each other, we were all we had. My grandmother couldn't have been any more conflicted. She loved my father like a son, but he was NOT her son and we WERE her grandchildren. She had to do what she felt in her heart was right, even if it killed her inside. Babies are innocent and need protection, she couldn't let us live like this any longer.

Chapter 10

The "Little House in the Big Woods"

-"Although this world is full of suffering, it is full also of the overcoming of it"

-Helen Keller

Shortly after dad took us away from our grandmother, mom came home from the Adventist Hospital. Mom and dad returned to drinking in record time, and the fights picked right back up where they left off. These fights were different than the previous ones however, Dad didn't have just anger in his eyes, he had hurt and pain, which I think made him even more dangerous. Dad would try to show restraint, but after the beating mom had suffered on Eldred street, she was a different person as well. I found some of her literature on co-dependent relationships, PTSD, and Domestic Violence. Then I picked up the AA book and I finally started to understand that my parents were both dealing with emotional and mental problems. It had nothing to do with lack of love for us girls, but deep seeded emotional problems they had of their own.

My parents quit seeing their psych doctor when he told them that my mother became psychotic when she drank alcohol. He said that psychosis is the overwhelming urge to have sex or fight with somebody. Mom refused prescription medication, she wasn't crazy! The person my mom was however, wasn't the person she was when she finished her psych/dry out stay. My mom was honestly never the same since she took that blow on Eldred Street. My mother's drinking and her anger escalated, and when she would get to a certain point in her drunken state, her eyes would glass over and she would attack my father. She flipped roles with my dad, and through no fault of his own, he reintroduced her to his former self.

My mother would park her nails in his throat, punch him, pull his hair, whatever she could at the time. Dad would take it, and cry, and beg God to take him home because he didn't want to be that person again, he didn't want to hit her. My mother had gone from being the victim to being the abuser. My dad would take the abuse as long as he could, but after he could take no more, he would punch holes in the wall, growling! That is also something I still dream about to this day. I knew when my dad made that terrifying sound, and punched holes in the wall, it was bad. There was death in the air, and he would return to beating mom's face in. Back to the black eyes, broken noses, split lips, although this time, he wasn't getting away with it without some war wounds of his own! This was around the time I referred to him locking my mother outside in the winter. There were many holes put into the wall as a result of my dad's violent rages. He constantly brought up my mom's previous affair, he called her "whore, slut, bitch" and blamed her constantly for him losing his job. I hear voices at night to this day, I hear my mother calling out for help, and when I was young, I was always there.

My mother would use my baby sissy and I for human shields, because she knew my dad would never strike us girls. I spent many nights feeling so tired I could drop, but fighting the urge to close my eyes, in fear of someone I loved dying. Once again, this was normal, right? Everyone went through this right? Or am I finally crazy? No time for questions, because we don't discuss family business with anybody. I never shared my family secrets with anyone, instead, I plunged into my books. I chose novels to Barbies, and hiking boots to heels. However not letting it out, not alerting an adult, in some way, to this day, makes me feel responsible for the decline in my family, for the future violence, for the future evictions, for the lost jobs, for all of the heartache that could've been prevented, had we received some family counseling. Maybe I wouldn't have died that night, that my Dad broke my mom's face, maybe I wouldn't have dropped to my knees when I saw the pain in my father's eyes when my mom dogged him for going from a hired associate at Hiroshima, to scraping gum off of the bottom of the drive through at McDonald's to support our family, and keep us together. Why did they never realize that my sissy and I took every blow, right along with them, hurt with every hurtful word said to each other, we were so little, and yet we were taking the beatings right along with them! Why couldn't they see that?

Chapter 11

"Loose toads and a baseball bat"

"There is not a righteous man on earth who does what is right and never sins."

-Ecclesiastes 7:20

I have a bittersweet memory of a place my parents took us as children. We called it "The Brook" in all actuality, I later in life learned it was called "Royality Creek." It was a fenced in park, with a little playground, and a beautiful brook of water running through it. It was so very beautiful, and the neighborhood children had built a damn so big, it filled the end of the creek so deep, there was a big tree log you could swing from a rope and jump off into the water. I have many fond childhood memories at this brook. We had cook outs, spent hours playing in the water, playing on the swings, and the little rusty merry-go-round.

My sissy and I would play for hours, splashing with mom & dad, and just having unbelievable family time. However, it was at this safe, family place, that I finally learned the connection between alcohol, and my parent's fights. On the way to our brook, mom and dad would stop at the store, get sissy and I a surprise, and get themselves, their "special drink." You see I had two sets of parents, the ones who took us to the brook, and the totally separate set of parents that took us home from the brook. I remember the last visit I made to our brook as a child. Unfortunately, now that I'm all too familiar with alcohol, I realize that my parents were drinking Vodka. I also realized that every time they drank this, they became possessed. Something was different about their eyes, their speech. It was like a story I had read called "Dr. Jeckyl and Mr. Hyde."

This made me hate the public from then on. It was such a traumatic embarrassment because my parents would scream, cuss, and sometimes my mother would destroy our barbeque by throwing the meat off the grill into the grass, and destroying our picnic-table. That's was ok though, I could find meat that wasn't dirty, and make sissy a hamburger. I couldn't have this, my sissy and I didn't deserve this embarrassment, we were just little kids, we didn't drink that alcohol-stuff. Besides, I was already a misfit in school, I couldn't let more people see what a Freak I was, and what my family was like in real life. If this got out, my baby sissy and I would surely have been taken to foster homes. One day, it was extra hot, and Dad had worked lots and lots of overtime to finally get us a car of our own again. We went to the brook for a couple hours and when we left, we went through the drive thru of a local fast food joint. This was an EXTRA special treat for sissy and I because although my father worked very hard, we were very poor. So, my mom was pretty drunk, and she began picking things off her burger she didn't like. My mother threw a piece of her then soggy hamburger on the clean carpets of my father's car he had worked so hard for. Granted, it wasn't new, but he worked his ass for it, and it was ours. So, he asked the "million- dollar question..." "Were you born in a fucking barn?" This always hurt my mother's feelings, so to get back at my father, she threw that soggy piece of burger to the floor of his car, and smashed it into the carpet with her feet. My mother then, took the rest of that soggy burger and shoved directly into my father's face, smashing it into his nose, eyes, everywhere! My father immediately grabbed my mother's head, pulling it down into his lap, and ripping her out of her seat. He then hit her over and over with closed fists and both hands directly in her head, and in her face. Then he grabbed her by the throat and squeezed until her face turned purple. As her eyes filled up with tears, and began to bug out, as her face was turning black, he let her go.

My sissy was screaming! She dropped her food on the floor of the back seat and was covering her eyes, then she once again began to scream for my Daddy to stop, all the while pulling her pretty little baby blonde hairs out of her head by the handful. I covered my sissy's eyes and pulled her out of the back seat. My mom, hair completely matted from daddy pulling it, slid out the passenger side door of the car, and found her balance on the outside of the car. My mother then began kicking the outside door of our new car, denting it. My father got out of his side of the car, and chased my mom into the house. By this time, sissy and I had already run inside, my father tackled my mother by the front door, grabbed her by the hair and began punching her in the head.

THE MONSTER INSIDE OF ME

My baby sister grabbed a baseball bat in a failed attempt to save our mother, and hit my dad in the head with it.

This didn't phase my father, instead, he grabbed the bat from my sissy and hit my mom in the head with it. There was only one door to get into our small apartment, and mom & dad were blocking it, so I couldn't get out to get help. My mother's screams gave me the adrenalin I needed to jump out the very high living room window, and run to the neighbors for help. By some miracle, my mother was able to break away from my father, grab my baby sissy, and run out of the house. My father locked the apartment door, and refused to come out. At this time, the neighbors were involved, the man next door plunged a snow shovel through the window, in an attempt to hit my dad with it. My dad was crying, freaking out. He was in mid-blackout, unaware of what he had just done.

The police showed up, they contacted our landlord and got the spare key to the apartment. They police entered our apartment, tackling my father, and putting him in hog ties. My father was screaming for my mother, no recollection of the events that had just taken place. My dad was taken to the county jail, and charged with a felony assault on my mother. Two weeks later, my father was released on bail, and was issued with a "No Contact order" for my mother. So, instead of renting a hotel room like we had done in past situations, my parents bought a family sized two room tent, and pitched it my Grandma Well's backyard. We camped for half of the summer until my dad's charges were dismissed. "No Witness, No Crime" I learned this term at a very young age. When my father was released from jail, he asked my mom to recall the events of that day, for he had no memory of them, "Damn Vodka!" At this point in my childhood, I had no illusions about the real world, I fully expected my dad to go to prison for blacking out and beating my mother to death. I thought back to my bucket of baby frogs that had got knocked over during this fight, and they got loose. I was more worried about what happened to my babies than the fact that my mother had just been beaten with a baseball bat. So, this is when I began to keep my most prized possessions and a nice outfit for sissy, a blanket and a baby for her in a suitcase under my bed, to be prepared, because the next time we had to leave, I refused to leave behind the very few things in life I loved. To this day, I am 35 years old, and I keep a "back up" bag under my bed...just in case.

Chapter 12

"A little Elbow grease, and the Monsters in the Windows"

"The torture of a bad conscience is the Hell of a living soul,"

-John Calvin

My very first opinion of "Tidwell Street" was not so good. I was skeptical on the idea of no more moving. We had moved seven or so times, and I was so socially awkward it was tragic. Although I super excelled in academics, I had no real friends, but you really don't have time for friends when you are an adult living in a child's body. You are so beyond the scope of conversation about cartoons, and trapper-keepers. You have a baby sissy to protect, and two live wires for parents. The only thing you DID have time for was keeping people away, so nobody would know how different your family really was. You had already lived with these secrets so long, and you have a responsibility of loyalty to the people who gave you life. My parents, my sissy and I thought of ourselves as the "Fantastic Four." All we had was each other, and nobody in this world could brake our family apart. "Sometimes Mommy's do things that upset

Daddies, and sometimes, Daddies have to put Mommies in sleeper holds for her own protection. This was normal, right?

As we walked through this house, it was awful! There were car parts under the kitchen sink, there was an empty refrigerator in the dining room, there were holes in the paneling and the drop ceiling was collapsing. There was a 40-gallon drum collecting waste dripping down from the upstairs bathroom. If we could clean up this place and give it some love, we would finally have a home of our own. No more moving, no more walking into a new classroom with eyeballs everywhere, we would have a fresh start, and maybe now I will find a best friend! We could create new memories, good ones. We could put the terrible past behind us. No more blood and booze smells, no more of Mommy calling Daddy names, pulling his hair, and digging into his neck! No more of Daddy kicking, punching, and squishing Mommy until you could hear her ribs crack, and the air leave her lungs. No more of Mommy's desperate screams, begging for her life. Our nightmare was over. In my young little mind, I was angry with both of my parents. I was angry with my Mommy for being crazy, attacking Daddy while he was driving on an iced over bridge on a cold, Michigan night, with my baby sissy and I in the back seat. Sissy grabbed ahold of my coat and yelled "Help, me Sissy!" To this day, I get sick to my stomach when I cross a bridge, or ride on the highway. As the weeks past, the house got cleaned out, enough for us to spend our first night. Our first night would prove to be very disturbing to me.

THE MONSTER INSIDE OF ME

My mother made a cozy warm bed for sissy and I on the floor of the upstairs, middle bedroom. There was an eerie, uneasy feeling in this particular bedroom. We curled up facing the two upper windows in the bedroom. These windows were so high, my father had to stand on a step ladder to put the tiny curtains up to them. It was so warm in the house that mom cracked the little windows, and kissed sissy and I goodnight. I drifted off to sleep quite quickly, but was awakened by a disturbing dream. A dream that turned into a night terror, it woke me up. I was paralyzed! I couldn't move, I couldn't scream, I had no air. It was such a vivid dream, it was actually real to me. My eyes burst open and there they were...my grandparents. My father's parents...Mr. And Mrs. Wilhoit! They were ghosts of some sort, but they looked evil, they were hovering in those high windows, their eyes burning red, the rest, solid black! They looked like demons, and then they said those words to me that I will always remember..."Get Out of the House!" I had never met my grandfather in person for he died before I was born, and my memories of my mother were very vague. Mostly chewing tobacco, and Christmas cookies. I knew it was them! There was no need for an introduction. I woke myself up screaming. My mother ran into the room and frantically shook me into reality. That night terror haunted me for years. Was it a warning? Maybe.

Anyhow, mom's drinking increased, and over the years, her anger and violence increased towards my father. My mother became a very dangerous alcoholic. Once again, I had a dilemma...who should I be upset with? My mother was becoming less and less of a victim, and more and more of the aggressor. And the time passed, I grew more and more numb to their fights. I learned to move out of the way and let them duke it out. Somebody would get knocked eventually. I could only hope.

There are certain fights, memories, and noises that still disturb me. And one question that still puzzles me? My father was the lead singer of a band, and his band members were always at my house. Why didn't anyone step in and stop their fights? My mother took beatings that would've killed a grown man, until one too many kicks or punches to the face made her snap. But at the current point in my life, I was too tired, too confused, and frankly, just stopped giving a shit about figuring out who to be upset with, who to be angry with. I was already tired, I was already an old soul living in a young body. I got to a point that at eight years old, I prayed to God to take mine and my Sissy's life, so we could go with that pretty black angel who visits me. I wanted sissy and I to go to a place that we weren't afraid anymore, where sissy wouldn't cry and pull her little baby hair out, where it just wouldn't hurt anymore. Or take my parents to Heaven, before they end up in Hell. Show me the way, and I just might do it myself. However, I would soon learn a valuable lesson, be careful what you wish for.......

Chapter 13

"Is the Tooth Fairy a Demon?"

"Nothing is permanent in this wicked world-not even our troubles."

-Charles Chaplin

One good memory that stands out in my mind is my mother's beautiful smile. She had very big, very white teeth. She had one little eye tooth that protruded, so she was very insecure and often covered her smile. As I learned at a young age, it seemed my mother's fate was to be an extremely unhappy woman. Now there are certain images that stand out heavily in my mind. However, there were so many beatings, choke spots, black eyes, split lips, and on top of that, not telling our "family business", I lost all hope. My mind became so jumbled, I couldn't determine the difference between what was real, and what was programmed. Which brings me to this specific chapter about my mother's teeth.

One night, she was wearing her maroon nightgown with the gold glitter moon. Something was wrong, for this was the nightgown she would crawl into after a fight, when she was too beat up to put on regular clothes. On top of that nightgown, I could smell it, stronger than ever...that horrible nightmare smell, blood and booze! Even worse, mom was moving at a snail's pace. I remember she had a bowl of chicken noodle soup, walked very slowly over to the couch, sat her soup on the t.v. tray, and very carefully, took her place on the couch. When my mother looked into my eyes, I couldn't believe what I saw. My mother had always been a thin woman, and what I saw in that moment would scare the Hell out of me, but make me extremely angry to this day. My mother looked terrifying! Her entire face was completely rounded, both eyes were swollen almost completely shut, and her entire face was bright purple, green, and even red! That was the end of my mother's beautiful smile, and the exact moment I promised myself I was either GOING to hurt a man one day, or I was going to help women like my mother escape monsters! I knew then and there, I was going to save a little girl one day afraid to go to sleep, keep her from ever knowing the smell of booze and blood, keep the "Quiet" from scaring her.

My mommy's pretty teeth were all smashed and broken off, she didn't look like my mother, she looked like something that was dead and forgot to lay down! Now, here's the explanation I got..."Your mother started drinking wine early in the morning. She drank through the whole day, she drank an entire gallon, and by the time she showed up at my band practice, she was shit faced. As soon as her feet hit the ice, she slipped. Being as intoxicated as she was, she was unable to put her hands out and brake her fall in time, before landing on her face, and smashing her teeth." But the story I heard in my young, jaded mind was, "Your mother showed up shit faced to practice, made a fool of herself, and it embarrassed me. I hit het and that was the end of her teeth, I knocked her "chicklets" down her throat!" I will never know the truth, but I have a good idea……

Chapter 14

"Never give an Irishman Liquor, because what happens next, is not "Magically Delicious."

"God sends meat, and the Devil sends cooks."

-*Thomas Deloney*

Now, across the street from this house we were trying to turn into our home, lived a man with a serious drinking problem. This man we knew still lived with his mother, he was Irish, he was an alcoholic, and an excellent mechanic (at least for the start of the day, before he became intoxicated). After this man got drunk, he was pure evil. The whole neighborhood knew about him, his name was Vance. It seemed like mom and dad were constantly going back and forth drinking with him. I always knew I was in for a long night when Vance would stumble across the street with his trusty bottle of Vodka. The fights between the three of them were brutal. My parents would get into a rumble with Vance, resulting in enough black eyes to go around for the three of them. Later they would cut ties for a couple months, then the cycle would start all over again.

Vance's mother was all of 4'8", and Vance had been a Vodka drunk since the age of nine. The children in our neighbor knew this tiny little fire cracker as "Grandma Leigh." Grandma Leigh was a widow, an enabler to her son Vance, and just an all-around helpless, weak woman. She did have a good heart however. Grandma Leigh was a serious martyr, and allowed her grown son to live with her rent free. This woman set no rules, no boundaries for she was terrified of him. Through no fault of her own, she enabled her son's severe addiction. Grandma Leigh invested thousands of dollars in rehab treatments for her son, but the fact of the matter was, he did not WANT to get sober.

After we moved into our "fixer upper", Grandma Leigh grew found of my father. During her son's black out drunks, she would call my father to come over to her house and put her "Chipmunk" to bed. A childhood nickname that stayed with him into adulthood. For years, this back and forth behavior would become routine. All of these "adults" would drink together, then Vance would sucker punch my mother or father (depending on his mood), and he and my dad would fight back and forth. Someone would bleed, they would fight back and forth until someone got tired, then they would give up and hug, or someone would go to jail. It was always scary to see my dad and this man fight, they both had martial arts training, and men don't pull hair and scratch. They crack heads, and break bones! My poor tiny mother always seemed to be caught in the middle. You see, Vance's brother was married to my Aunt Leddie, and was also the father of my three cousins, and that's how Vance was my uncle. Vance made a couple of references in front of me that I picked up on, so I went to my mother and demanded an explanation, and if I was old enough to know the truth or not, I was in for a major dose of reality!

Chapter 15

"The truth shall set you free..."

"Wordsworth wrote, "A simple child/That lightly draws its breath/And feels life in every limb/What should it know of death?"

I have very little memory of the late 1980's, but the memories I do have are nuts! The year was 1987, and in the era of men wearing spandex pants, more eyeshadow than their wives, and enough "Aquanet" aerosol hairspray to gas you to death, my dad was an inspiring musician. He was signed by a small record label, and I took his record to "Show and tell" in my kindergarten class. Dad was always gone at work, he worked in a factory, and was gone all the time. When my dad was around, he had lots and lots of friends over all the time. This was the year I would never forget, it was the year my mommy and daddy got married. My mommy would finally have the same last name as sissy and I. This was also the year however that my dad almost died, and the year my mom paid for the mistake of putting sissy and I in the car, and attempting an escape with us girls. It was going to be me, mommy, and sissy. This would also be the year that I would learn to associate sirens with daddy hurting mommy. To this day, I cover my ears, and get tears in my eyes when I hear sirens too close. We had a small house on Lowland Ct., and what I learned later about this house was that this was where my dad lived when he was a junkie. Mom had already gone through the needle addiction with him. When my mom found out she was pregnant for me, she gave my dad a choice, it was the needle or me. And in the grand tradition of most of us addicts, he traded one addiction for another.

With cocaine still being my dad's drug of choice, he discovered a brand-new way of getting high, a way my mother would NEVER figure out. It would keep him going, keep him productive for work, and then he would stop, this would not be a forever thing, just enough to get him through. My father discovered "Freebase." My dad had learned how to smoke cocaine, no more needles, although he would miss that instant gratification, that warm rush that made the hair on his arms stand up, he didn't need it anymore, because this was much safer! This particular drug habit, would soon adopt the term, "Smoking Crack." My dad was now cooking his own cocaine into rock form and smoking it! Four and a half months later, this habit almost took his life. My dad was working twelve hour, seven days a week in a hot factory, and was dabbling with cocaine in his spare time. He learned how to make a little extra money and smoke for free. His health started fading, he became sicker and sicker. Despite all of my mother's efforts, he just kept getting worse. The next thing I knew, my father was in the I.C.U., fighting for his life. My mother was forced to make a judgement call, and his doctor told my mother, if my father could have stood the pain another 24 hours, he would not have survived. When my father was finally stable enough, his doctor confronted him, and asked him the "million-dollar question"…"Mr. Wilhoit, have you been using, rather smoking rock cocaine?" My father denied it at first, then his doctor went on to say, based on his diagnosis, and the results of his tox screen, he knew the answer already. Then the doctor explained to my father how lucky he was to have his life, and exactly what was wrong. The doctor then showed my dad an image of his heart. My dad's heart was much larger, and was surrounded by what looked like a white cloud. The doctor went on to explain to my father that his heart was almost triple it's normal size, and the white cloud around his heart was a viral infection of his pericardium (fluid sack around the heart) better known as "Pericarditis". This particular condition, given his young age, and tox screens confirmed the doctor's suspicion…my father had a sever cocaine problem. My father spent eleven days in I.C.U. and then was released to come home to his family, quickly ending his love of cocaine. He confessed everything to my mother…. he finally came clean.

Chapter 16

"Grand Theft Auto"

"A woman must not depend on the protection of a man, but must be taught to protect herself."

-Susan B. Anthony

My last memory of that house on Lowland Ct., is what pushed me over the edge and sparked my absolute paralyzing fear of the sound of police and ambulance sirens. I don't remember what caused this particular fight, I just remember the aftermath. Dad had been beating on mom throughout the day, and now that I think back with an adult mind, I realize he and mom had been drinking all day. When dad passed out, mom snuck sissy and I out to the car and said she was taking us to see Aunt Maggie. Aunt Maggie had a house in the country with a big windmill in the front yard. Aunt Maggie's house was like a whole other world. I'm not sure what scared me more, the thought of mom being beaten to death, or the thought of her driving me and sissy with no glasses and swollen eyes. (Mommy is legally blind without her glasses) on top of that, mommy doesn't know how to drive, she has no license. Mommy got sissy and I all

THE MONSTER INSIDE OF ME

buckled in, got into the driver's seat, and then it hit her... oh shit! She forgot to grab the car keys! So, mommy told me to keep my sissy safe, and promise her, no matter what happened, I wouldn't get out of the car. I knew right then and there, that my mommy wasn't going to leave that house in one piece. I don't know how long sissy and I were in the car, I do know however that it was bright and sunny when we got in the car, and there was a colorful sunset when the police officers pulled us out of the car. Before that, I had an eerie feeling. When I heard the sirens, I knew my mommy was either coming out of that house dead, or looking scary. Either way this played out, I had a job to do, to protect my sissy. So, I filled her sippy cup with juice from her diaper bag, ran my hands through her pretty blonde hair and over her chunky little face, closed my eyes, and waited for those sirens to get closer. To this day, I don't know who called the police, this was long before cell phones, but I knew that even though the sirens sent chills through my little bones, help was on the way.

The ambulance was on the way. The ambulance pulled up right after the police officers pulled us out of the car. My Grandma Well pulled up directly after. My grandmother told us girls to get into her car, and fasten our seatbelts. I tried to stall, because I wanted to see my mother. All of the sudden, there she was. My mother was strapped to a stretcher with her neck in a brace, and gauze over one side of her head. I could see the blood seeping through the gauze. I just lost everything inside of me, I fell to my knees, I felt like my life was over. Grandma Well took us home with her and made us grilled cheese and tomato soup, she was so fun, she gave us little fishy crackers and chocolate milk to go with it. Now that I thought of it, I hadn't eaten yet that day. Now if my memory serves me correctly, my Grandma Well told me that my father had beaten my mom in the head with a heavy object, and bitten her ear almost completely off of her head. Then Grandma explained to me that I had to take good care of my baby sister, because all we had in this life was each other. I told myself that I would spend my life with cats instead of boys. Cats were fluffy and purred, boys hit you, and called you names. With all the fights I witnesses, I came to the realization that fairy tales were just stories, and here in real life, there were NO happy endings.

Chapter 17

"Why Can't I Breathe?"

Author Christian Nestell once wrote, "No man is happy without a delusion of some kind. Delusions are as necessary to our happiness as realities."

Time passed, and things started to get better. The work on our new home was moving along quite well. I was beginning to feel a bit more secure in our living situation. One night, I spiked a fever, and started to vomit. I developed a dry, non-productive cough, that tickled my throat and tortured me for hours. The vomiting was so bad, "Oh great, I have the flu." My mom made a bed next to her on the couch and put a cold washcloth on my head. My dad made multiple trips to the store for me, chicken soup, Gatorade, Tylenol, cough syrup, you name it! Nothing was helping, my health rapidly declined. My mother pushed fluids, tried to get me to eat, rubbed vapor rub under my nose and across my boney chest, she refused to leave my side. They next day, my cough progressed, and after 24 hours without a wink of sleep, my parents got me in to my pediatrician. The doctor told me mother that I had bronchitis, and sent me home with my very first nebulizer, and narcotic cough medicine. This remedy did not help me however, my cough increased, my vomiting increased, the pain when I breathed was indescribable! I became lethargic, and gasped for air. A simple trip to the bathroom was impossible. My grandmother dropped off a commode to keep next to my bed. I was so skinny, so fragile, and so weak, my family feared the very worst.

One morning, after a long, long night, my chest became very, very warm. My mother was sitting next to me on the couch. The noise in the room became muffled, and the scent of lilacs filled the air. All of the sudden the aroma of brown sugar took over my senses, and she was back! That beautiful angel with the black wings! She was peeking over my mother's shoulder, as my mother sat next to me, rubbing my head. My body felt light, and she reached out her hand for me. I reached out to take her hand, when all of the sudden my hearing became so sensitive! "Jack, she needs to go!" I heard my mother saying. "Hold on baby, we are going to get you some help" my mother said to me. My parents had no car at the time, and we had no health insurance. My mother called my Grandma Well, who was at our front door in two minutes! My grandmother lived two blocks around the corner. The next thing I knew, I was in the back seat of my Grandmother's car, and my father was speeding us to the emergency room. "Go away pretty angel! I'm not going today either! Things are better, we have a home now, I'm starting to like school! I think I'm going to have friends pretty soon! You can't take me away!!!!" She sat in the front seat in between my parents facing me, just looking into my eyes. "Why can't anyone see you?" I was dying. I leaned my head back, and everything got really bright!

The crash team moved me to the trauma room and cut my clothes off. They put all types of needles and tubes in me everywhere. "Why are you doing this to me? I want my Mommy!" I was later admitted and diagnosed with Asthma, and Micro-plasma pneumonia (Walking pneumonia) I didn't understand what was wrong with me, and truth be told, neither did my doctors. This was just the very small beginning of what I feel my future was not supposed to be. Over the next few months, my E.R. trips and hospitalizations became routine. My weight dropped to a dramatic 60 pounds, my skin was pale, and often grey. By the age of 10, I had already suffered from collapsed lungs, had been air lifted to another hospital and endured more pain than most grown women did in a lifetime. I was consumed by the thought of death, and for the second time in my young life, I questioned God. "You are NOT going to die", my mother whispered in my ear, as the tears rolled down my face, during yet, another seven-day hospital stay. "I won't let you, God can't have you yet, Dana Leigh." I smiled at my mother, I had to, I had to show her that I was NOT afraid. Deep down though, I couldn't be any more terrified. It seemed as if that pretty black angel had taken up permanent residence in my life, and it didn't look like she was leaving anytime soon. I could do this, I could ignore her, I would just focus on my baby sissy, as I had often done in the past.

Chapter 18

"A kidney transplant, and a sad, sad Christmas"

"We all die. The goal isn't to live forever. The goal is to create something that will."

-Chuck Palahniuk.

The seasons changed, and I started to come to terms with my newly discovered disease. Two doors down from my family, lived two heavy set girls, who had just suffered a terrible loss. That past Christmas, they lost their mother. These girls were so sweet, and had the biggest hearts, and their mother had been sick their entire life. Their mother was a Type I Diabetic, who survived a kidney transplant only to die a month later from a massive heart attack. After their mother's death, they moved with their father to his mother's house two doors down from us.

Although their father loved them very much, he had no idea how to help his daughters cope with their mother's untimely death. So, he showed him love in the best way he knew how.

He gave them sweets, and money. He never talked to them, never checked on them, never showed interest in their academic activities, nothing. I believe he never really knew his children.

One good thing I can say about my parents, was aside from their alcohol problem, they were extremely supportive of our academic achievements. We got to know these chubby little girls, there was Marcy, the oldest, and Ashlynn, the youngest. Marcy took on the role as mother to her baby sissy. Marcy and I grew close very quickly, for we both knew what it was like to put our needs to the side, and tend to our sissies. Marcy fed her sissy, picked out her school clothes, helped with homework, and tucked her in at night. Marcy did everything a good mother would do for her child.

It wasn't long before my first real friends witnessed the secret I had been carrying for years, my parent's "Episodes." What surprised me however, was these girls grew to love the four of us as if we were their real family, and chose to be a part of our family dysfunction vs. Going home to a "emotionally anorexic" father. I feel that Marcy felt a sense of motherly responsibility for sissy and I, and I soon went from no friends at all, to two more sisters. Maybe there WAS a God after all, and he was finally making time for my sissy and I.

Chapter 19

"A very special Christmas, and a nurse I'll never forget."

"I think the truly natural things are dreams, which nature can't touch with decay."

- Bob Dylan.

My life had become a constant roller coaster of emotions. Mom and dad would have their cycles. The house would be clean, dinner on the table, and no fighting for weeks, and just as I began to relax..."BOOM!" The vodka would return, and so would the fights. Mom and dad were still taking turns beating on each other, it was a complete toss of the coin as to who would be crazy that night. Sissy and I were much bigger now, we had sadly come to the conclusion in our young little minds that "Happiness is not automatic, it is a gift, and gifts weren't necessarily for everybody. Enjoy it while it lasted, because at any moment, it could be gone again."

My mother would verbally bash my father, she would strip him of his manhood right in front of us girls. My father would cry, and beg God for forgiveness, and try to hug my mother. My mother would return this gesture by scratching and spitting in his face. Then my dad would remind my mother how ugly she was, and how no other man would put up with her drunken scenes. Both of my parents grew up with fathers who would emotionally abused them, tell them they had no worth, why couldn't they see that saying these hurtful things to each other was just killing my baby sister and I! Every time my parents shed tears at the hands of each other's abuse, a little piece of sissy and I died inside.

I often asked myself, "How, just how can you hurt the person you love? After my diagnosis, this would only be the beginning of a life changing, auto-immune disorder. My future asthma attacks were very violent. There were combined with severe seizures, neither myself nor my family were prepared for what our life was ultimately going to turn into. Long stretches of hospital stays, rounds and rounds of painful tests, an oxygen tent, a helicopter ride to the hospital the next city over. My childhood became a dream of playing outside with my sissy, but a harsh reality of confinement to a hospital bed. "Not today pretty angel! Quit creeping around my room! I'm not going anywhere! My mommy will make me better, you watch!" My body was getting weaker, and it was getting easier and easier to give in to these violent attacks. I would lose my bodily functions, I would be paralyzed, able to hear, but unable to respond. I was petrified! And SHE wouldn't go away, that Beautiful angel. I figured out she was "Death" and to this very day, she has been around, my entire life.

My doctors told my parents at the rate these violent attacks were going, I would not live to see the age of 18. This was my fate, "what did I do to deserve this? Was this a punishment because I questioned the very thought of a God?" Was I being punished for the violent person I really was inside? No! I love animals! I started a food drive at my school for kids who were hungry! I wanted to grow up and be a nurse! I wanted to help people! I wanted to write a book one day! Screw you Death! I will beat you, or you'll have to take me kicking and screaming!" My attacks struck when I fell asleep, I began terrified to sleep in fear of dying. For the first time in my life my Mommy & Daddy came together and weren't fighting lately! I spent more time in a hospital bed than I did at home. I began to feel homesick for the hospital when I was home. Did I have "Stockholm Syndrome?" I had read about this. I had my school work brought to my hospital room, I would except NO special treatment. I won awards for my scholastic achievements I won the "Presidential Academic Fitness Award! I received a big gold medal for this. My teacher would visit me in the hospital, she was my friend. The other kids didn't understand, school was my everything! School was going to take me to a better place, I just had to live! I had to fight.

I'll never forget the last Christmas I still believed in Santa. I was eleven years old, and stuck in the hospital on Christmas Eve...alone. My parents were bringing my sissy first thing in the morning to see me. I couldn't be selfish, my sissy deserved Santa to come for her. She was still a baby to me. She needed to sleep in her own bed, she was so little! I stayed strong on the phone with Mommy and Daddy, I told them goodnight and told my baby sissy I loved her. As soon as the phone call ended I broke down so bad, my doctor ordered me an I.V. sedative. I was so innocent, I believed Santa was going to forget me because I was not home in bed with Sissy.

I woke up at 3:00 am on Christmas morning, and called for the nurse to help me to the bathroom. I was so weak, I could not drag my I.V. pole without help. Low and behold, there it was! I couldn't believe my eyes, the most beautiful sight I could imagine. On my side table, there they were...two stuffed bunnies, hooked together by a hug. One brown, one white! There was a tag on them that said "Love, Santa." And then, across from my bed, against the wall, a rocking chair! This rocking chair was not there when I had fallen asleep. It was covered with strings of lights, garland, and around were so many Christmas presents! They were all wrapped up, so pretty. There were presents of all sizes, all colors! "Santa didn't forget me after all! I better get back to sleep so I can wake up to the best Christmas present imaginable... my baby sissy!"

Chapter 20

"The invisible girl"

Mario Puzo wrote, "The strength of a family, like the strength of an army, is in its loyalty to each other."

My hospital stays consumed my family. Our lives had become nothing but sleepless nights in the E.R., missed work, and fear of sleeping. My parents were so occupied by supporting me through my painful hospital stays, they, through no fault of their own, began to neglect the needs of my baby sister. I was so self-absorbed with proving I was not a "Freak of Nature" I too, slowly drifted away from my sissy. She was so little, walking to school alone, bringing my homework home to my parents, and spending her time worrying about her big sissy, that I don't feel she ever developed her own identity. She was always "Dana's little sister."

By this time in my life, I was thirteen years old, and I was starting to beat the odds! Everything I accomplished was such a miracle, "Hell", I was a miracle. My parents tried so hard to fill the void of the disappointments in my life due to my illness, that I honestly believe, accidently became emotionally unavailable towards my baby sissy. Every time I got sick I told myself that was the price I had to pay to have any sense of real family.

As time went on, and the initial shock of my disease wore off, my parents returned to the booze and the fights. What I know now that I wish I'd known then was "How do you deal with the stress of worrying if every day with your child, might be your last?" The only thing on my mind at this time was wondering how I was going to protect my baby sissy? I didn't want to be selfish, so I kept in the need to understand if my family understood that although the hospital looked fun, it didn't come without sacrifice, without pain, without anxiety so bad, my chest was breaking! But they had enough on their plates, I would keep this to myself.

The steroids I had to take to keep me alive were starting to take a toll on my body, and later in my life would create a "Domino Effect" towards my spiraling health. I spent years being completely disappointed in this "Wonderful, all-knowing, all-loving God" my parents always spoke of. If God was so loving, "Why did he allow such pain, such hurt in my family? Why wouldn't he take away my parent's alcohol addiction? Why wouldn't he give my father the job he deserves? Why was my family so poor? And the question I struggle with to this day is "What the Hell did I do to deserve such a painful disease? Why am I so sick? When am I not going to be a freak of nature anymore? At that point in my young life, I gave up praying. Praying never kept my mother safe. Praying never took my sickness away. It was then and there that I came to the conclusion that "God" was no more of a story than "Santa."

It made no sense to get on my sore, skinny little knees, and pray to a "God" that I couldn't see or hear. I began to challenge anyone who attempted to talk religion to me. The more my parents pushed this issue, the more I challenged them. I thought about it like this, "I believe in what I can see, hear, taste, touch, and smell." That made sense to me. I needed an explanation. I wanted to believe in "Fairy Godmothers" as well, but that did not make them real. To this day, I believe in medical science. I've been legally dead several times, and did I see the pearly gates? No! Just that damn angel with the black wings right before I drifted off to sleep, smelling lilacs. The feeling that I experienced when my heart stopped was indescribable, and at times in my life, I yearn to return to. The feeling of peace, of no pain, of just letting go. To lose your bodily functions and lean back into that warm bowl of jello. An overwhelming sense of calm filled my tired little body. All of the pain, panic, fear, anxiety, everything, just gone, and I drifted to sleep.

Before I could fall completely to sleep, I would hear a crash! The lights were so bright in my face, and their where doctors all around me fighting for my life. Had they possibly understood the wonderful place they had just taken from me, they wouldn't dream of returning me to the cruel, sad, painful world as I knew it. Throughout my life, I have revisited that wonderful place, but have yet to be able to stay, for I have a sissy, a family that love and need me. I think about my sissy and all she's been through and it makes my heart very heavy. I need to protect her, all we have is each other........

Chapter 21

"Is addiction really hereditary?"

Gandhi said, "I have seen children successfully surmount the effects of an evil inheritance. That is due to purity being an inherent attribute of the soul."

I remember when drinking first became a problem for me. One day, I found it! The pint of Vodka my parents had misplaced the night before. I was 14 years old. I grabbed a glass of orange juice, took them both to my room and sat on my waterbed. "What was the big deal about this evil drink? I had already seen evil, and I was tired. There MUST be something good about it, why else would mom and dad keep drinking it? I opened it, smelled it..."Yuck!" How could they drink this garbage? At this point I felt I had nothing to lose, my curiosity took over. "Bottoms Up!" I took my first shot, Down the hatch! My stomach got very warm. Suddenly, I wanted another, and another! Before I knew it, the pint was empty. Music had a whole new meaning! I wanted to blast my stereo, I wanted to write, I wanted to sing! I wanted to dance! I fell to seep on my bed, the next thing I knew, my light popped on and my mother was waking me up for school. I had had my first blackout experience with alcohol, but I felt great! I found myself more and more often drinking alone, all alone in my room, with my stereo and my pen & paper! I finally understood it! If you just drank little bits, alcohol was great! It gave me confidence to conquer the world!

It didn't take long before my parents busted me. Given my fragile health at the time, they didn't know what to do. So, they made a decision. Instead of me sneaking around, and risking an attack around strangers, or the risks of someone taking advantage of me, they decided to provide a safe place for my friends and I to drink under supervision. Unfortunately, 90% of the time I drank, I blacked out and could not recall the events of the night before. Suddenly, I had so many new friends, and threw lots of parties.

Everybody wanted to hang out at my house. In fact, one of the protective parents who inspected one of my parties before dropping a class mate of mine off, a man with a family, later in life became one of my very most dependable "Sugar Daddies!" (But that's for book Two!)

My black outs increased, and became violent. I drank, blacked out, made a fool of myself, and woke up guilty the next day. One time, I woke up face down on my bedroom floor, all of my pretty glass collectables I had saved since early childhood, were smashed! It looked like a tornado had hit my bedroom. I had no recollection of the night before. Surprisingly, my mother was very understanding, and tried to gently walk me through the events of the night before. Apparently, as usual I drank too fast (I have always been a "power drinker"), attacked my parents, and said the most awful things to them. After my outburst, I cussed "God" out, threw up, and passed out. I was so very ashamed of myself. Although my father meant well, he showed me how to "kill" a hangover, by taking a couple shots of the same booze I drank the night before. I should have paid better of the warning signs, but I thought I could control my drinking. After all, I had strait "A's" in school, and I decreased my drinking to Friday nights only. I refused to turn into my parents. That was impossible! I was in control! Besides I couldn't be an alcoholic, I was only fourteen.

Chapter 22

"The Blue-Eyed Devil"

Thomas Kempis wrote, "Love feels no burden, thinks nothing of its trouble, attempts what is above its strength, pleads no excuse of impossibility; for it thinks all things lawful for itself, and all things possible."

High school was extremely difficult for me, but I had my very best friend, Danielle. We walked to and from school together. I was a member of the High School orchestra, being the "Principal" cellist (First Chair). I walked across town every day, with that big beast strapped to my back. When I played my cello, I escaped into an entirely different world. The music traveled through my body and penetrated my soul. I was free, I was creating beautiful music. This, and my creative writing class was what I got out of bed for every day. Unfortunately, however, I had more classes to attend than that. As I traveled the hallways, I was overcome with paralyzing anxiety. I kept my eyes to the floor. When guys tried to talk to me, all I could picture in my mind was the memory of my experience in the "Doll Corner".

And I refused to be the family dog again. I refused to have all of those beautiful blonde girls make fun of my curly hair or the holes in my shoes. That was not me anymore! I had long burgundy hair, braces, a slim figure…"just breathe", I would tell myself. If I kept my head down and didn't see everybody looking at me, I could get to my next class, and sit down. I understood music, and I understood creative writing. In those classes, I could be me. One day, I saw the most gorgeous blue eyes I had ever seen. His name was Duke. Duke was the most gorgeous, sweet, caring, intelligent guy I had ever come in contact with in my life. When he got close to me, I would "breathe him in." Every second I spent with him was so special, because that was exactly how he made me feel, "special, pretty, wanted, appreciated." We would talk on the phone for hours, sometimes we would still be on the phone from the night before when my alarm would go off for school the following day.

I didn't care though, I didn't need sleep, I had someone in my life that made me feel like a person. We made our relationship official between my sophomore and junior year, and within just a couple months, I ran away from home and moved in with him. I met his mother in the most unconventional way. I had stayed the night with her son, in her house. My worst fear came true, after one of the most wonderful sexual experiences I had ever had, I made the mistake of falling asleep naked. And then it happened, I had a seizure! Right there in her house, in her son's room, there I was flopping around on the floor, naked as the day I was born. She somehow managed to find my parents, and everybody met me at the hospital. I was taken by ambulance.

I was so embarrassed, I had lost my bodily functions and everything. She came into the E.R., peeked her head in and called me a nickname I treasure to this day..."Little Bird"

Her name was "Patty", and she was so beautiful. She looked like a real-life Pocahontas. She was very tall, with strong Native American features. She had the deepest brown eyes, and the kindest smile. Patty and I hit it off very quickly, we became fast friends. She was very supportive of my education, my job, and absolutely loved that I loved her son. Like me, Patty was also suffering in silence with a terrible disease. Patty had cancer. She knew what it was like to be sick, she was someone I could talk to, someone who didn't make me feel like a freak. On top of this, her son and I were very much in love.

The next year would prove to be one of the best years of my life. I grew closer and closer to Patty, and I had the most unbelievable times with her son. We threw parties, he took me for walks at night time, he was so proud to have me on his side. I was on cloud nine. Nothing could bring me down. The year was 1999, and I was in love! It wasn't long before I moved in my baby sissy, though she was far from a baby. Her and I were so close, she dated a friend of Duke's, and the four of us had an amazing summer. Fast forward to New Year's Eve, 2000. Patty had kicked Duke out when she discovered he was stealing from her. Like the loyal girlfriend I was, I went with him. Actually, Duke moved his things into my parent's house. He was working at an auto shop owned by a family friend. In the back of this shop he had a wave-less waterbed, big screen t.v., and video surveillance around the entire property. I knew this to be a fact, because I had stayed there with him overnight in the past.

As 5:00 hit, I gave him enough time to shower and he was supposed to come pick me and our friend "Mismack" up to begin our New Year's celebration. I had a surprise for him, I had finally come out of my shell and bleached my hair blonde. I was naturally a dark blonde, but due to the memories I had of the girls who tormented me in school being blonde, I kept my hair a very dark burgundy. I had finally done it, I was blonde.

I was all dressed and ready to see him, but to my surprise, he hadn't called. I must have rung that shop phone 20 times over the next two hours, I didn't understand, something was wrong. I phoned Mismack, and that's when my whole world came crashing down. Mismack told me Duke had to work on his ex-girlfriend's car, who he had been seeing behind my back. I instantly threw up! This couldn't be true! Duke and I were in love, and on top of that, we were best friends. We did everything together, we talked. I told him my deepest, darkest secrets. "What had I done wrong?" I demanded answers! I just wanted to know why? Why did he betray my trust? Why did he lie to me? I didn't lie to him! It wasn't supposed to be like this! We were going to get married one day, I was going to write a book, and we were going to have a big beautiful house! This was absolutely unacceptable! I screamed and yelled until I lost my voice, when he finally got on the phone with me, he wouldn't explain himself, he was completely cold, and all he could say was he didn't love me anymore. I had held nothing back, gave him every ounce of love and trust I had, and this just wasn't enough. This was my first broken heart, and I had never felt a pain or betrayal like this before. I promised myself, I would never put myself in the position to feel this pain again. Now, I'm 35 years old, and still haven't loved in the way I loved him. My dad tried to give me advice, but who was he? He didn't know love like I did. Duke and I didn't fight, he didn't call me names, we respected each other.

The worst part of this heart break was the thought of losing his mother. How could he bring such a wonderful person into my life and then rip her away like that? Truth be told however, his mother never left my life. Though there are periods of time we do not hear from each other, when we reconnect, it's like we didn't miss a second. She will always be a very special person in my life.

Chapter 23

"And yet to every bad there's a worse."

-Thomas Hardy

It was now late February, and my parents both worked third shift. Following my break-up, I made it a point to surround myself with every guy I possibly could, full of blood lust, and ready to attack. So, one night, my sissy and I threw a tattoo party. I was getting my first of many tattoos on my upper right leg, and HE walked in. He was the Mexican drug dealer from the old neighborhood, seeing him in the light this time, he sort of resembled a chihuahua. I had seen him once or twice when I went with Duke to his house to buy some pot. This was before my drug days ever began. Here he was, standing in my bedroom, watching me get this tattoo. I paid no attention to him at first, he didn't really catch my eye, for he was nothing special, and only somewhat easy on the eyes. After the party started to die down, and I was running out of booze, he pulled out a brand new fifth of cognac. He popped the cork, and finally caught my attention. He tried to be confident, but he was no match for me, and within an hour, we were all alone in my bedroom, and he was pouring his little heart out to me. It was different to see this side of him. It was a big difference between sitting under the tree in his front yard with his pit bull, smoking a blunt, than talking my ear of, drinking shot after shot. Then it happened, my first one night stand, and after I finally asked his name, and he told me. "Pablo, Pablo Martinez."

About 4:00 a.m., I kicked everyone out, including Pedro. Sissy and I had to clean the house before mom and dad got home. Then in my drunken mind, I had a thought, "Screw that!" I'm not cleaning a damn thing! Let mom and dad clean up after us like I had done so many, many times after them. As time went on, I became more and more detached and longed for my own place. I started seeing Pedro, although I had no intensions of ever calling him back. He was like a little puppy dog, begging for a treat. He grew on me, he was always there, always around. Then one night, Duke called me to go to the hot tubs, he wanted to "catch up", while I was on the phone with him, Pablo beeped in, so I went with my gut. I had Pedro come pick me up. "What the Hell right? What did I have to lose? He took me to his mother's house and we parked out front. We went walking, and something happened, he was a different person. We did not drink, but we engaged in deep, meaningful conversation. After Pedro dropped me off at home, he went home and told his mother that "I was the one! He was in love!"

I contacted my old boss from the nursing home I used to wash dishes in, and inquired about the nursing assistant class. Due to the fact that I had been a very dependable employee, that never turned down overtime in the past, she agreed to put me through the course. It was held at the community college.

I was still in high school, but decided if I could slip between the cracks and enroll in a college course, then why would I waste my time in high school? If I could go straight to my dream job in two weeks. I longed to touch the lives of people who gave us ours. I wanted to work in Hospice. I couldn't think of a time in my life that I wanted anything more. So, the nursing home paid for my training course at the community college. So, I was in class eight hours a day, and worked nights in a nearby deli. I had tunnel vision, I wanted this certification, and nothing was going to stand in my way. It was nothing personal against my present co-workers, but I wanted to do more than just punch the clock. I wanted to leave work with the satisfaction that I made a difference. I set another goal for myself, to make as much money as I could, doing the very thing I loved, caring for the elderly. I was good at it, I could discuss mortality with someone who understood me. I could connect with people that were balancing between life and death. I couldn't talk to Pedro about any of this, for his scope didn't go very far beyond the bottom of his cognac bottles. It would be years before we had another meaningful conversation, for I was his arm candy, and he was my rebound man, nothing more, nothing less. He once told me he understood, he wasn't Duke, but maybe he could grow on me, this made me feel very bad for him, but I gave it a shot. Throughout my life, I have always felt like I was in Limbo, waiting for the next level, for something bigger. All though I still had feelings, it was difficult to tap into them. To this day, when I feel, I feel like there is a space between, just enough, that I can't quite reach out and touch what's real...

Chapter 24

"Return of the warm jello, and now I am invisible..."

"If it is a miracle, any sort of evidence will answer. But if it is a fact, proof is necessary."

-Mark Twain

Time went on, and my heart began to heal. It was a slow and unbelievably painful process, but with the support of my family, and Duke's ex-best friend, "Bill", things seemed to get better. I wasn't crying everyday anymore, and Bill seemed to be a positive distraction. Duke and I had rented a room from him in the past, however due to Duke's addiction to stealing, he was put out. Being the loyal girlfriend, I was at the time, I stayed by his side. Bill and I had both been in toxic relationships, and we began to start seeing each other. One night, he took me to a very nice restaurant. On the way there, I got a rush of shivers, and an overwhelming sense of doom. As I lowered the mirror on my sun visor to reapply my lipstick, I saw her in the back seat.

The angel was back! I pretended I didn't see her, I had an internal conversation with myself. "Nothing is wrong! Shut your eyes, and focus, and she will go away!" This was a prime example of self-sabotage, and it wasn't taking me under!" I had just learned to doggie-paddle that summer, I was facing my fear of the water, she wasn't going to come creeping back around and take me anywhere!" At dinner, I ordered a hamburger, fries, and a root beer. To my disappointment, I was unable to eat. It was so strange to me, I was hungry when I got there, but then felt so physically full that I was unable to eat. This "full" feeling, turned into pressure, and it spread from my tummy to my whole body. I had to unhook the button of my tight leather pants, which was odd to me because I was very lean and in shape.

After dinner, Bill and I went back to my parent's house. All of us sat down to the dining room table to start a card game. As we all were talking, their voices began to echo, and feel far away. Next, my vision changed, the table became smaller and smaller, and then I saw something so very beautiful. I glanced to the wall beside me, and then to the ceiling. There was beautiful silver glitter falling everywhere. And then there she was...the angel. The silver glitter had gathered on her big black wings. She stood up, and opened those beautiful wings, wrapped them around me, and I instantly felt it. I had the most beautiful euphoric feeling I had ever experienced! I was in complete Utopia, she was taking me to that place. I had finally given in to her, I had let go. I had no idea what was in store for me next, but the room was full of lilacs and brown sugar, my pain was gone, I could FINALLY breathe. To my surprise, I was in peace, so I shut my eyes and drifted off to sleep. The angel was rubbing my head like my mother used to, and I knew right then and there, she had won!

The very next thing I remember, I must've been in a bed, because people were standing over me, talking to me as if I wasn't really there. I was talking to them, but they weren't listening, in fact, they couldn't even see me. I stood up in a panic. "Why are they doing this to me? Why are they ignoring me? What did I do wrong?" I tried to get their attention by waving my arms around and yelling. I then noticed something that made my blood run cold. They were ALL staring in the same direction, behind me. I spun around, and horrified, I saw it, I saw myself in a hospital bed. I had tubes coming out of my body, two in fact, pumping blood out of my chest. One of these tubes, were down my throat breathing for me. I collapsed, because then I also saw her! The angel was sitting on my body, wings wide open. She had tears rolling out of her eyes, and she kissed my forehead. It had finally happened, I was dead, and had gone to Hell. A place I never had believed in, was now my harsh reality.

Next, I was back in my body. I was paralyzed. I was unable to talk, unable to reach out, unable to communicate to my family that I was in there. My cousin "Angie" was standing at my bedside, she was running her long nails through my hair.

It felt so good, she talked to me. Angie was so beautiful, wearing her sunflower outfit. It was jean shorts, with sunflower pockets, and a white tank top, covered in a sheer top with sunflowers all over it. Next, I felt a violent pain in my chest, and up my throat. It was the tube that had been breathing for me being removed from my chest. My mother explained it to me like this…I had experienced a "Bilateral Pneumothorax." Meaning I had such a severe asthma attack, my lungs blew holes in themselves. My lungs then filled up with blood and I suffocated. In turn, I was placed in a medical induced coma, my lungs had been opened up on both sides, and chest tubes had been inserted to drain the blood and relieve the pressure. I had then been placed on a ventilator, so my lungs could rest and heal, while this machine breathed for me. The doctors had told my family that the chances of me waking up were very slim. If I had awakened, due to the amount of time my brain was starved of oxygen, it was unlikely, that I would ever be the same. When I was able to speak, I told my cousin Angie what I had seen. My nurse who was standing directly in front of me broke into tears, and told me that was impossible. You see, due to the pressure in my body, my eyes were taped shut throughout my coma to prevent them from popping out of my head. I have no explanation for what I saw, but the fact of the matter is, I DID SEE IT!

I had done nothing to deserve this, I suppose I should've been thankful for surviving this ordeal, but a part of me to this day, feels I was robbed. You should not mess with the natural order of things. Though I am grateful for my life, I have never felt right sense then. I feel as if I am in an alternate universe. It was this event that unleashed some of the anger, and confusion I still battle with to this day….

Chapter 25

"Misdirected Hate"

"All things truly wicked start from an innocence."

- Ernest Hemingway

After my coma, I grew more hateful, and had come to the self-realization that there was "No God." If there had truly been a "God" he wouldn't have let me grow up seeing so much violence, it just wasn't normal. It wasn't normal to catch your father screwing your mother's sister, it wasn't normal to live without heat or hot water, or to carry buckets of water from grandma's house to flush the toilet with. I feel like I lost my soul in that coma, for I've not been complete since then. I was a prisoner. When I came home, I was far from grateful, I had lost my self-respect. My focus drifted to hurting every guy that crossed my path. For a while, I did. Why not? I was beautiful, right? It was just a shame that my insides did not match my outsides. I would take a date to a party, and purposely instigate a fight. Why not use my manipulation to hurt a guy? Surely, a physical shot from me would be no match, so, "work smarter, not harder."

I tore friendships apart, humiliated and be-little'd these guys, turned them to my own "Personal minions of destruction." I felt powerful, although at the end of my day," I still cried in the shower. It was safe, nobody would know. Nobody would see the tears roll down my face. Nobody would see me stuff the washcloth in my mouth so it would muffle the sounds of my screams! And I screamed so loud! I sat in the bottom of the shower and cried. "I cried for every time I saw my mother with a black eye. I cried for every time my dad broke into tears at the sounds of my mother telling him how worthless he was. I cried for the memory of my sissy tearing her little baby hair out! I cried for that angel who tempted me with the thought of a place where these visions go away, and then ripping it away from me! I cried that nobody knew I was crying! I cried until my eyes hurt, until I couldn't take my heart ripping from my chest, but most important I cried for the fact that I had been robbed of what was supposed to have happened! I was NOT supposed to survive that coma! It wasn't right! Why was I here? What was my purpose? Deep down I was still a freak, still ugly, still that little girl who was the "family dog" in the doll corner, still escaping into books, still ashamed, still scared, still crying out for help, still disappointed, still let down, still invisible." I wanted my Mommy, I didn't want to be me!

I stopped in from time to time to check on my parent's. My dad had lost his job, a great job, a wonderful job at a local cereal factory, for the stupidest reason. It wasn't fair!

He was doing good, providing for my mother. He had morphed into a completely different person. He had rediscovered his manhood, found his pride, was doing excellent. At the time, my Dad was in a band. He had been performing on the weekends during his days off from work. He had a show coming up, so in the office at the factory, he ran of copies of flyers of his upcoming show. He was so proud, so excited. What he didn't know, was that he worked with a jealous, rat, whose name was "Lonnie." My father had accidently left the original copy of his flyer in the copy machine at work, and Lonnie discovered it. Lonnie proceeded to push "99" on the number of copies, turn on the overhead light, and close the door. He did this so the boss would walk into this mess first thing in the morning. Needless to say, my father was terminated from his job, and has struggled ever since.

Chapter 26

"Things do not change. We change."

-Henry David Thoreau.

Note to the Reader,

Now, I am going to fast forward a bit, and although there are certain events I would like to include, I have to respect the privacy of my baby sissy. I will just say this, "My baby sister's life has been no picnic, especially taking into consideration what we survived as children. Against the odds, my sister is a very strong woman and wonderful mother. To me however, she will always be the sissy I stuffed into the back of my little car and rode down the hill with. She will always be MY BABY SISSY!

Chapter 27

"All work and No Play..."

"Everybody wants to go to heaven, but nobody wants to die."

-Joe Louis

By this time, I started to calm my ways a bit. I had moved Pedro into my apartment, and tried to focus on getting my life together. I had passed my nursing assistant course with a 4.0, and received a perfect score on my test for State Board Certification. I came home to a very special reward from Pedro...and GIANT teddy bear and a card to celebrate how proud of my accomplishment he was. This was a very special time in my life, for I loved my job so much. But at the end of the night, due to the insane hours I worked, I neglected my sister, my family, and Pedro. I wanted nice things and a comfortable life. I found myself becoming obsessed with buying laundry soap and toilet paper, in fear of running out. Sometimes, my closet would be completely full of these items. I was finally doing it! I was providing for myself, and doing a DAMN good job of it! I was doing this by myself, and

I learned to give "the bird" to that stalking ass angel invading my apartment. Hadn't she learned by now, that she wasn't getting me? I had zero trust, and zero faith in Pedro, but I could see that he had something good deep down inside. He had something special and one day, I was going to tap into it. Not today however, today is ALL about me.

Now, I don't know if it was the smell of my success that attracted Duke back into my life, but BAM! Here he was again! You see Duke had a dream of what his life should be, but truth be told, he felt he was entitled to skip working from the bottom to get it. He was my drug though, a link to my innocence, something I could never resist. I loved to be high on his very presence, I admit it, I was guilty. At this point however, I was conflicted. True I would never have that lustful animal attraction for Pedro that I had for Duke, but Duke had left me behind. He left me all alone, and Pedro had picked up the pieces. I think I was looking for something in Pedro I would NEVER find. I was looking for that first love, that first crush, that beautiful presence that he would just never be, he would never be him, he would never be Duke, and I punished him for this. Though I had no illusions that Duke was done whoring around, I couldn't help myself. I was hypnotized by his beauty, I had bit the apple, and I was ready for eternal rest.

After a short time tasting that forbidden fruit, I had to make a choice, and I chose Pedro. Pedro made sense. Pedro was loving and safe. Though I was not "In love" with him, he had grown on me and I honestly felt I could grow to love him. Pedro had earned my trust, my respect, and before I knew it, we had become best friends. I had discovered a whole new kind of love, and I spent many, many years with him.

Chapter 28

"Can I let go Mama? I'm so tired, I don't want to do this anymore..."

"Some of us think holding on makes us strong; but sometimes it is letting go."

-Hermann Hesse

I was lying in a field of lilacs, with the sun so very bright, it was heating up my face. As I struggled to open my eyes, I couldn't shake the overwhelming sense of Euphoria! As my eyelids lost this vicious battle to the sun, I slowly closed them. As my body began to float away, it happened! BAM! I was hit by a truck! Not actually, but it felt like it. When I landed, I landed in my own body, and when I was able to open my eyes, I was strapped down to a hospital bed, with nurses and doctors all around me. A doctor was holding my eyelid open with one hand, and shining a light into it with another. "What drugs have you taken ma'am?" And then the sun returned, as well as the smell of the lilacs, and there she was, my angel, like clockwork. "BAM!" The truck hit me again, this time throwing my body very far. When I landed, I hit so hard the air left my lungs with so much pain. I opened my eyes just in time to see the nurses rush in with the crash cart, and all of the supplies need to intubate me again!" Not again! Please! I can't take it again! Where are my children? Where is my sissy"? What is my name? Why don't I know who I am? "Ma'am, you have overdosed on heroin, and now we are going to put you on a ventilator so your lungs can rest, please don't try to talk..."

Then I began to dream, or was this a memory? I was sitting in my truck, outside the doctor's office I used to work at. My life, my mistakes, my failures all filling my mind at a terrifying rate! It was like a tidal wave crashed into me. I had failed everyone who had loved me, my children, my family, I was a total waste of space! I am so ashamed, how did I let it go this far? It was never supposed to be like this, I wasn't supposed to be a junkie! Omg! What have I done?" I grabbed my dull syringe full of that thick, brown, sweet poison. Where could I hit? My hands, my arms, my feet, even my breasts were all black and blue! So, I turned the rear-view mirror towards the only spot I had left, my neck! I looked for a pulse, then I drove that dull needle the best I could deep into that vein and plunged it! I just wanted to sleep, I wanted the pain to stop! I didn't want to be poison to the people I loved anymore. Their lives would be better off without having to worry about me. No more worrying if I was going to show up stumbling drunk, or nodding in my cereal bowl. No more pain, we were all going to have peace. "Ma'am, what drugs have you taken?" Then my mind drifted back to better days. In the times before social media and cellphones, my mother made everything an adventure! Like the time her and my dad found an old CB Radio, my mom would laugh as she created the handle "Clean arm pits" and would laugh with the truckers on the road.

Or how she would let us girls completely take over the living room building forts, and she would fill our tents full of munchies as we watched "Pippi Long stocking", and" Chitty, Chitty, Bang Bang "over and over. Or how when the "Care Bears Movie" would interact with those of us watching at home. They would ask us to join hands, and with all the love in our hearts say the words with them "We Care" over and over. My mother would join hands with us, and magically "Christie would escape the influence of "Dark Heart". It really felt like the love and energy our mom shared with us as we gripped her hands so tight really worked! We were "Care Bear Champs" all because of my mother! But I was no "Care Bear Champ" anymore, the fact was, I was a junkie, and a drain on society, and on my poor mother! "Ma'am can you hear me? Can you open your eyes?"

Chapter 29

"Where there is death comes life...."

"Live so that when your children think of fairness and integrity, they think of you."

- H. Jackson Brown, Jr.

Thinking back, Pedro and I had a rocky relationship. I was self-absorbed, trying to live everyday as if it were my last, all the while neglecting Pedro in the process. I have to admit, I blame myself for the "Cold Hearted Motherfucker "he is to this day. My focus was on money, I wanted to make as much as I could as fast as I could, I was 20 years old and had my entire life ahead of me. I had passed my nursing assistant course two years before, and worked with everything I had since then. I transferred to Hospice care. I bonded with my Hospice patients immediately! I understood them. I couldn't discuss mortality with people my age, because unless they had seen the evil I had, they would have absolutely no idea! One of my little ladies that molded the caregiver I used to be, I will never forget. This beautiful little lady was a "DNR" meaning do not resuscitate. She had refused pain and anxiety medications. She had cancer, and she was rotting from the inside out. In a very short six months, I saw her go from a feisty silver fox (who refused her tomato soup, unless it was in a glass bowl, on a plate, surrounded by Ritz crackers) to a skeleton, resembling a Holocaust survivor. She could no longer communicate beyond her moans and cries, she was suffering. This beautiful woman I would spend hours talking to after my shift, had declined so very fast. I watched her revert back into a child, sleeping with her baby dolls, soiling herself, and depending on us nursing assistants for her total care. "We come into the world bald, toothless, and soiling ourselves, and we leave the exact same way."

I loved this woman as if she were a part of my very own family, and in a sense, she was. I spent sixteen hours a day, six days a week caring for these people, and they just fade away, right in front of your eyes. When you spend this much time with people they become a part of you, you love them, protect them, and shed tears for them. I sat at her bedside for days, turning her every hour, rubbing ice chips on her lips, putting cold cloths on her head, doing everything my mother had done for me. She moaned in pain, as I watched her clutch her rosary, I began to wonder "Did this woman really have this much faith, this much love for an invisible "God" that was leaving her to suffer?" I couldn't even fathom the thought. This woman was a good, Christian woman, with enough faith for the both of us.

Her family had dumped her in this HELLHOLE! They quickly cleared her bank account, and changed their telephone numbers. She came to us very positive, although severely abused. I had become the only one she deemed worthy of caring for her. She bit the others, and flicked feces at them, urinated on herself, but none of that with me. She shouted racial slurs at the others, and refused care from them. Due to my deep tan, and dark curly hair, she assumed I was of mixed ethnic background. I can recall the exact moment I earned her respect. I came on shift and received my shift report. Apparently, my little lady had been extra "Spicy" that night. She had been beyond combative, shouting racial slurs. When I entered her room it reeked of urine, she, along with her bed was completely soaked. I attempted to clean her up. She scratched me and called me names. I said to her, "Shame on you! I am trying to help you. Or would you prefer for me to leave you this way? It's your choice." She immediately released her grip in my arms, and said to me "Go ahead, I really don't give a damn anymore!" I proceeded to clean her up, change her sheets, and tuck her in. She grabbed my arm, looked me in the eyes, and said something that makes me chuckle to this very day..."Honey, even though you're a dirty Negro, I love ya." I had to respect her honestly, and on top of that it made me feel honored. You have to understand, these people are from very different times, things were so, so much different. You can't take it personal.

As her health declined, she had severe mood swings, but something was different. Something did not sit well with me. When she had come to my hall, upon admission, I noticed a change in her behavior, and an obvious abnormality in her right forearm during her skin assessment. I immediately scanned her chart and saw that the social worker suspected abuse. I called my nursing supervisor. We got an order for mobile x-ray. Low and behold, there it was. She not only had multiple healed over fractures, but she had a current spiral fracture in her forearm. This only confirmed my theory, this woman had been abused! Spiral fractures in the forearm occur from someone twisting your arm! So, I frantically asked my nursing supervisor to request some pain medication for her. Much to my surprise, I was informed that she was already presently receiving pain medication. "Bullshit!" I checked her chart, and it was charted that the nurse from the shift before had been administering her pain medication every four hours. I lost my breath! I knew this woman well, and you would have to slip her pain medication, which I highly doubted anyone had done.

I could also tell by her frequent urge to urinate with no success, she had a U.T.I. I checked her intake and output record, everything was charted as "normal." I called "bullshit" again! She had severe skin breakdown, and multiple pressure ulcers (bed sores). Her skin assessments didn't make any sense! Nothing made sense to me! I could feel the vomit rise up in my throat! I was so upset tears filled my eyes, and I felt that anger inside return. I wanted to crack heads! All of her narcotics had been initialed by a nurse I considered my mentor. I took my evidence to the director of nursing, and she immediately issued a drug screen for my little lady as well as the nurse whom I loved very much. And what a big shock, my little lady was negative for opiates, and my nurse manager was positive. This nurse was immediately terminated, and escorted from the property.

I was immediately promoted to preceptor (team leader). My job was to validate all of the charting for the other aides on my hall. I was ordered to have them join me for bed checks at the end of my shift as well as join them at the beginning of theirs. I certainly didn't gain any friends of my co-workers, in fact, I became a "Lepper." I didn't care though, it was worth it. I didn't care to gain friends, I just wanted to protect these people! Back to my little lady...here she was, eaten up with cancer, rotting from the inside. Suffering! In the end I stayed right by her side. With all my double shifts, I had but eight hours in between. Two of which I slept in the chair next to her bed. And then one night, I heard it, the "Death Rattle". If you've ever heard this, it would burn a permanent image you would never forget. It took every bit of energy I had not to put a pillow over her face and end her pain. "How could her "God" let her suffer so badly? I would never understand this "God" people devoted so much valuable time calling out to, only to be left alone in the end. Scared, alone, full of pain and suffering. I wanted to be her "Angel of Death" I wanted to push that final morphine shot that would give her all the peace she deserved. I thought of Jack Kevorkian, and understood. She had fluid in her throat and she was gurgling on it. She was fighting, crying out in pain, moaning, just fucking suffering! I felt impotent! I was completely helpless! And then I smelled it, a smell I was all too familiar with...lilacs and brown sugar. Suddenly the gurgling stopped. A sense of peace filled her face. She had a small smile on her face. She began to mumble and point, she was talking to someone. She lifted her skinny little finger and pointed behind me. I turned, fully expecting to see my nurse manager in the doorway. There was nobody there. I turned my attention back to my little lady. She gave me the most beautiful smile, squeezed my hand, and exhaled. Then she looked right through me, and her pupils dilated. She was gone. She died at 3:01 am, and I found myself crying happy tears. "When we lose the people we love, we find that we do not shed tears for them. We are crying for ourselves, because WE will never see them, but I assure you, they are in a better place".

A few weeks after I lost my little lady, I found out I was pregnant for my first daughter. Where there is death, begins life!"

Chapter 30

"The gift I didn't know how very much I wanted, until I got it..."

"If I am what I have, and if I lose what I have, who, then, am I?"

-German psychologist Erich Fromm.

I didn't understand how I could be pregnant. I had been on a birth control shot. This was, by far, one of the scariest things I had hit me head on! "What kind of mother would I be? Could I survive a pregnancy? Would my steroids effect my baby? Oh, my God! How did I find out? It's actually funny, looking back on that day....

I had taken my mom to lunch at a nearby drive thru. I ordered a fruit punch. After I drank it, my stomach burned like fire, and I vomited. I called the manager, and began to cuss him out. Then my mother had a revelation, I had to be pregnant. I had become moody, and cried often (which was rare, I didn't normally cry in front of people). "No way!" I said, that is impossible! I'm on the shot! So, I made her a bet. There was a Planned Parenthood two blocks away from her house, if I was "preggo", I would buy the next lunch. Five minutes after I peed in that cup it was confirmed! I was going to be a Mommy! "What would Pedro say? Would he leave me? Would I be one of those single mothers with a biracial baby. I had no idea of his Spanish heritage, or how they raised their children. My head was spinning, none the less, I was happy.

I continued to work at the nursing home until, I experienced problems with my pregnancy. During my 7th month, I got so very sick. Bleeding, anemia, and pneumonia. I spent more time in the hospital than out. I had a 45-minute drive to see specialists that took over my high-risk pregnancy, for it was beyond the scope of a regular OBGYN. At this point, my doctors advised an emergency C-section. They told me my baby would be cared for in the neo-natal in an incubator, until she finished developing. (Enters my future demon-in-law, Louise) She was completely obsessed with completely obsessed with this beautiful little Mexican child I was carrying. Perhaps she thought of it as a "do over" of her son that she had royally screwed up. She had absolutely no regard as to the quality of both the baby and my life, only her grandchild. She didn't care if I became a human incubator, harvesting a child, as long as she had claim to it. That would be just the beginning of her sick obsession with my children. I did the best I could, Pedro disappeared and I was alone. I had no idea where he was, or who he was spending his nights with. Nights when I burned with fevers, gasped for air, and was afraid for the life of our child. Pedro resurfaced one week before I gave

THE MONSTER INSIDE OF ME

birth. This innocent baby had no idea what she was doing to me. She was putting so much pressure on my lungs, it was literally killing me. I was admitted to the hospital for pneumonia. "Maybe this is what I deserved, to handle this alone. Lord knows I was ANYTHING but good to Pedro over the years. I had lied cheated, betrayed, and Humiliated him. He had been my "emotional tampon." Maybe it was payback time. I was doing my absolute best to hold her in. I was in the hospital for almost two weeks, when the doctors decided at the first day of my eighth month, they were going to perform an emergency C-section. They inserted Cytotek into my cervix. This was supposed to soften it, so my labor would begin. One pill every six hours. They walked me up and down the hall wearing oxygen. At this time this course of treatment was ineffective. Next, they started a Pitocin drip through my I.V. site. I laid in agony for what felt like an eternity, although it was actually only a few hours, I was losing oxygen saturation, and in my mind, losing my baby, and my life. "Take me! I'm a terrible person, but my baby hasn't even taken her first breath yet." I thought to myself. I hallucinated, vomited, and gasped for air, but I never yelled out. If I yelled out than this was real, and we were both dying! I wasn't giving that dark angel the satisfaction of offering me a way out, I was going to finish this, and if I died in the process, so be it. I realized right then and there, for the first time in my self-adsorbed life, that I loved someone else in this world more than myself.

Next, the doctor broke my water, and then the REAL pain started! My contractions felt like they were ripping my hips apart, I started to drift away from my body. The doctor checked me. I had only dilated to one centimeter. So down to C-section I went. I was placed on a ventilator, and sedated. My last memory was putting my hands on my big belly and falling asleep. When I woke up I returned my hands to my belly, but it was gone! "What the Hell? Where was my mother? She is always there for me when I need her. Then I smelled it. The cheap perfume my future demon-in-law sprayed on herself. AS I slowly adjusted to the bright lights of the hospital room lights I saw something that royally pissed me off! It was her, "Louise" holding my tiny, premature baby! And she was feeding her! Where in the FUCK was my mother? Why was this "Twatwaffle" who gave me absolutely zero support feeding my baby? Why was ANYBODY feeding my baby? She was supposed to be breast fed! I felt a knot swell up in my throat! At that exact moment I understood why cats would eat their kittens! My baby had been pawed on, washed, dressed, and fucking fed! "Unbelievable!" I wanted to jump up, grab my daughter, and knock that bitch's teeth down her throat! How could SHE be here? The demon who rolled her eyes, when I decided to have my baby delivered early. I had questioned this bitch's sanity early on, when I showed up to her house late one night, and she had been lying in bed with her then 11-year son. She was in her skimpy panties and half top that barely covered her breasts! Super inappropriate! When I got home with the baby Pedro didn't stay. He couldn't run out the door fast enough! I instantly dropped the diaper and broke into tears. Holding my mother as tight as I could! My mother instantly kissed her grandbaby!

THE MONSTER INSIDE OF ME

Now it was time for the "million-dollar question" Where were you when I needed my mother more than ever? You have NEVER let me down?"

My mother went on to explain. Louise had accompanied my mother downstairs while my mother smoked her cigarette. This was already odd to me because that bitch didn't smoke. But I tried to give her the benefit of the doubt, the grandmothers were bonding. Louise left to return to the floor about five minutes before my mother. Ten minutes after my mother returned to the floor herself, security approached her. They immediately escorted her out of the hospital. They told her they had received an anonymous report that my mother had been drinking vodka at the hospital and made direct threats towards a staff member. I was heated! I knew for a fact for this to be untrue. You see what nobody realized was that after two shots of vodka, my mother would have been a complete tornado at the hospital.

Another thing nobody realized was that I was very old friends with the head of security at the hospital, "Tony." He told me the entire staff was on edge about my condition. He told me Louise approached the security office, and said she had just left my mother outside. She said my mother pulled out a bottle of vodka from her purse, took a swig and put it back. Then she said my mother made threats towards a nurse on my unit. She said she wanted to keep this tip private, for she feared for her safety. So, security escorted my entire family, with the exception of my sissy, off of the property. How could that BITCH do this to me? To her grandbaby? She should've felt fortunate my mother HADN'T been drinking vodka, my mother survived my father, and no skinny little "crackhead" bitch was a match for her! She would've had those jaws of hers wired shut! Where was that demon when I was in and out of the hospital? Was she the one spending night after night holding my hair while I vomited? Was she the one putting towels on my head to break my fevers? Was she the one who stayed by my side when I went into adrenaline shock trying to come off of the steroids for my baby? No! Fast forward out two months. The visits from his side of the family became less and less. Who was there when I was recovering from my C-section with a compromised immune system? My mother! And she was honored to be! Who was there when my milk dried up, and I was crying along with my newborn because I was unable to feed her. Who was there when I was sleep deprived with a new baby with colic? Who got me help for my severe post-partum depression? My mother! Not that BITCH!

Louise would listen to my mother's ideas for gifts she could never afford for her grandbaby, and immediately run out and buy them for her. Through all of this hurt, through this betrayal, my mother still had a dream of co-grandparenting with this demon fossil. I have no idea why, but that's not for me to understand. My mother shook her off like a flea. She had no time for this very petty competition. She was above, and so very much more than that.

A note to my readers...

You will find that throughout my book, I jump back and forth through time. I ask for your patience, there is a method to my madness. Keep in mind, this is the first book of a trilogy, meaning I have two more books to bring my story together, and help it make some sense to you. I hope you are enjoying my story so far, I'll admit, it is a lot to take in. And as the tears are presently rolling down my face, please understand, I am far from the hero of my story. I just hope that after reading my trilogy, my story reaches someone out there. I hope it helps you to make better choices than I did. It has been a long, hard road. In the end, we are all human, we are all sinners. We play roles in our lives. At one time or another, we are all the child, the parent, the sinner, the villain, the aggressor, the victim, the manipulator, the Angel of Death, the addict, the control freak, and the one who repents. We are all human, and we have to fall, to make mistakes, and to regret to learn. I just hope some of you out there read my story and chose a different path for yourselves. You can do it, if nobody else believes in you, I do. Thank you for your support.

Chapter 31

"Can someone please arrest this psycho in the mirror? She is stalking me..."

Jean Racine said, "A tragedy need not have blood and death; it's enough that it all be filled with that majestic sadness that is the pleasure of tragedy."

I used to listen to a song about a "man in the mirror", but it took me years to comprehend the actual meaning. I had run-ins with that person from time to time, but as many times as I have tried to kill her, she continued to stalk me. I had transformed from that powerless little girl to a very cold, resentful, calculating, manipulative, cross-addicted, bitter mess! I went on week long alcohol and drug binges. I used every drug I could get my hands on. Unfortunately, however, no matter how much I smoked, drank, injected, snorted, booty-bumped, hot railed, or foiled, nothing took away that anger I had inside. I was a MONSTER! I had lied, hurt, lied, extorted, used, assaulted, and manipulated everyone I loved. I not only had burned every bridge, but I had dropped that "A-Bomb." From about the ages of 21-32 years old, I was an F-5 tornado, devouring everyone and everything in my path. I had sold my soul, but I often questioned if I had even been born with one to begin with.

I destroyed my relationship with my sissy, and her three children (Aunt Dana will get to you babies, don't you worry). I had lied to my soon to be ex-husband, hid my drug problem, used with his friends and family, had multiple affairs, I was awful. I wanted to own it, I was riddled with guilt. Where did I start? Every time his cell phone rang, my heart dropped! I just knew it was someone on the other end exposing my secrets. How could someone expose your secrets when you had insurance on them though? My marriage had run its course, by now, I had opened our bedroom to other women, to three-some's. I shared my husband with many women, I had lost all sense of self-respect. I was a loaded gun, ready to fire! I began to sell my body to pay the pills, at least that's how it started in the beginning. I had good intensions. I had a day job, but my "moonlighting" took a toll on my body, my-self-respect, and most of all my conscience. I soon found that I was making more money in an hour in my night job, then I did in a week, at my 40 hour a week job. My night job began to overlap into my day job, then before too long, I left my day job, and worked full time as an escort. I was able to pay my bills, keep food in the house, buy my children nice things. What I didn't realize at the time but, I was the one that had become "emotionally unavailable" to my children. I was so focused on making money, that I spent less and less time with my girls, and they spent more and more time with miscellaneous family members. Sure, we had beautiful and nice things, but I robbed my children of the one thing they needed the most, their Mama!

I began to have affairs with married men, men with fetishes. I was introduced into a whole new world. These men would let me put dog collars on them, walk them to my bathroom, and slam their faces into my toilet. Married men, that had secret lives separate from their happy home lives. Some of these men would see me multiple times a week, and exchange for fetish fun, would leave me donations that knocked my socks off. Manly men that would close my blinds and put on woman's lingerie, have me put them in bed restraints, and penetrate their rectums with huge, black strap on dildos! This did not stimulate me sexually, but I developed a kind of a "blood lust" craving the power to dominate these men. I would push them, inflict physical pain, plain out torture them. All to be left a donation, and they would go back to their boring wives. You see, I believe I saw my father in these men, and I wanted to hurt him, make him bleed, humiliate and degrade them, everything I feel he did to my mother. Then I had a revelation, I could live off of these donations! There was a market in fetishes, role play, testicle torture, pissing on them, you name it!

This is a very sick world we live in! When I first adopted this lifestyle, I feel I developed a split personality.

<u>Scenario #1:</u>

I would ask my dates, why they were there with me, and what they were missing in their life. One of my dates in particular, informed me his wife had recently had a hysterectomy and seemed to have lost her sex drive. He felt empty, lonely, unattractive, and unloved. I asked him if he ever considered if his wife had felt the same? He looked at the floor, and said it had never crossed his mind. I asked how often he was unfaithful, he said this was his very first experience with an escort. He said he sat outside of my house for twenty minutes before he knocked on my door. I told him not to make that mistake now. I told him to go and get a bottle of his wife's favorite wine, and her favorite flower (which happened to be daisies). Walk in the door, grab her by the face, look in her eyes and tell her how beautiful she is. Without holding back, give her the most passionate kiss he could muster. Have a glass of wine, then swipe everything off of the dining room table, and lift her onto it. Keep kissing her, reach up her skirt, and slowly pull her panties down. Gently spread her legs apart, and proceed to give her the slowest, most passionate oral you possibly can. Take a pause, tell her how sweet she tastes, kiss her again. Tell her how much you miss her, and keep up the oral, so slow, until she starts to quiver. Kiss it, lick it, torture her with pleasure. Run your nails softly up and down her legs, and up her tummy until you reach her breasts. Keep licking so soft, so slow, then find her sweet spot and pick up speed, and "Viola! Niagra Falls!" To this day, I receive a Christmas card in the mail, with a little cash, as well as a picture of the happy couple!

<u>Scenario #2</u>

If I happened to wake up that morning in a particular dark mood, I would see my date that liked my leather "Dom" outfit. I would lay out the toys, collars, paddles, nipple clamps, and other miscellaneous "torture tools." I drank a lot back then. I drank to numb my feelings, to kill my fears, to mentally prepare myself for what I had to do.

It takes a disturbed mind to cover your bed in plastic in preparation to squat over someone, and piss in their face. I had to be prepared, ready to dish out discipline, ready to give punishments.

This particular man was married, yet another over-privileged white man with repressed homosexual feelings. This man wanted me to punish him for fantasying about "Hollywood Hunks", just to gain the inspiration to pleasure his wife. So, I obliged him. I gave it to him good! I restrained his feet, applied the nipple clamps, and he just loved "Testicle Torture." He loved my feet in my roman sandals, so much in fact, he had me remove them and tie them around his testicles. So, I did, until they turned purple, you could damn near see his penis throbbing with his pulse. I whipped his back, cained his legs, burned his stomach with hot candle wax, he didn't care, he loved it. He wasn't worried about an explanation for his wife, for he couldn't remember the last time they had been naked together.

Then, the real punishment began, I flipped him over, tightened his foot restraints, reminded him of his "safe word" and got it done! I violently penetrated him with my huge black strap on that I referred to as "Kong!" He left a happy man, and left yet one more, more than generous donation. He had no idea, that when he left my house, he took a piece of my soul with him. I could smell the brown sugar, and she appeared in the corner of my bedroom as I rolled the plastic off my bed covered in feces and blood. She looked at me, and she shook her head. She appeared to have tears rolling down her cheeks. "What the Hell do you know anyways angel? You've been a cock tease my entire life. You have dangled the hope of a better place in front of my face so many times, it makes me sick! Why don't you pay for this humongous house, left over from my failure as a wife? Why don't you feed my children, while their dad leaves them weekend after weekend on my doorstep. They wait until the sky turns pink, my youngest falls asleep on her suitcase, and I carry her inside and put her to bed. Ny oldest asks me "why Daddy doesn't love her anymore? Questions that make my tummy burn, because I am supposed to protect her, and I have failed her. And worst of all I realize I am no better of a mother than he is a father, he just doesn't hide it. I'm the worst out of us both! Back to my room to indulge in more self-abuse, as I wait on date #3 for the evening. I have already had donations in the amount of $1,000 dollars for this evening, but I need more! Another shot, another blast, another rail..."Draino anyone?"

The last customer of the night, I will definitely go to Hell over. I had a gentleman who wanted the usual, torture, restraints, the usual. It was nothing I wasn't used to. He specifically wanted to be restrained face down, keeping his hands free for access to his phone. That was cool with me. He wanted the "Kong" treatment, but something was different with this one. He wanted to call me Daddy! Awkward, but hey, it was his hour not mine, and if the sick fuck wanted to roll that was, it was fine with me. As I was pouring the wax up his back, taking a quick break from "Kong", I happened to glance over his shoulder, and what I saw brings tears to my eyes to this day. He was looking at pictures of one of the most beautiful baby boys I had ever seen! This boy couldn't have been any older than three years old! I fought the urge to vomit. I asked him if he minded if I switch toys. He said it was fine, so I released him completely, reached over to my side table, grabbed my mace, and sprayed him in the eyes! As he screamed, I told him if his wife had any questions, she should feel free to give me a call. I'm sure my number was in his phone. I reached into his pants and took his driver's license so I would have his address.

I told him I was going to have some Nazi, "Murf freak" friends of mine keep a close eye on him and if he went ANYWHERE near a child, well, they would be more than happy to "Professionally disrespect his asshole", what I had just given him would be small potatoes, and I met every single word of it! Back in those days, I had some very loyal connections that would love to destroy a sick twist like that! I didn't worry about legal repercussions, for that would have been a rather awkward police report to file. What would he say "The escort I visited behind my wife's back, assaulted me for possession of "kiddy porn?" After this encounter, I went directly into the bathroom and vomited! I didn't know if it was the drugs, the alcohol, my nerves, or the combination of all three, but I didn't know how much more of this truly "sick world" I could take. I could write a separate book on my experience as an escort alone. I had been assaulted, robbed, blackmailed, extorted, you name it. I hated myself and the life I was living. I was completely dead inside, and I could literally hear "ticking" in my ears. I was not the crocodile in "Peter Pan" however this was serious. The sand was running out of the hourglass, and though there was no "Wicked Witch of the West to melt, I was going to "Kill that little bitch in mocking me in the mirror", if it was the last thing I did.

Chapter 32

"I must've been "Hitler's Mistress."

Marcel Proust wrote, "Remembrance of things past is not necessarily the remembrance of things as they were."

At this point in my story, I am the mother of two babies. "Malorie and Eva" They were both stubborn little preemies, but worth every second of it! I could never explain in words the feelings that filled my body both times I became a mother. How could a "Dead Woman Walking" like me, bring such beautiful little girls into the world? I love my babies, though, I can now admit to myself, I never quite deserved them. "Love" may as well be a four-letter word sewn on a pillow in some dusty yard sale box if you don't show it. I did my best, for I love my babies with everything I have left inside of me!

According to people in my children's lives presently, I must've created an "alternate universe" because my memories of my children are so beautiful, so happy, so, full of love. I will be the first to admit however, my children did witness some of my actions in the depths of my addiction. Like me, I repeated the pattern of exposing my children to situations they should've never been in, and to this day, my baby doesn't know me, and my oldest wants nothing to do with me. I did this to myself, and have nobody to push the blame on. My heart hurts every day, and hopefully, one day, my children will want to come to me for answers.

As I recall, I had two beautiful, little young ladies who were so full of love to give. We would have our "girl time" we would curl up in bed together, and they would fight over who would lay closest to their Mama. How my youngest baby was such a grouch in the morning. She would yell "Shut up birds!" When the birds chirped outside her bedroom windows. How this funny little baby of mine had such an old soul, she couldn't begin her day, or even hear someone's mouth, until she had her morning cup. (In her case, her milk sippy). Or how my curious little baby walked in on my drying off in the bathroom after a shower and asked me "Mama? Are my boobs going to get long like yours one day?" She was so funny, spunky, and full of life. She once told me she couldn't pick up her mess in her playroom, because she had "Tiny hands."

My oldest baby was also a very old soul, who could prepare a nebulizer treatment for her mama before her first slumber party took place. She was so sweet, and made it her job to lay her sissy down for her naps. I often saw myself in my oldest daughter. She would sing to me with the most beautiful voice, I had ever heard. My life took such a downward spiral, I had to walk away from my children, for their own good, as well as mine. Pablo was in a stable place, mooching

THE MONSTER INSIDE OF ME

off of his new girlfriend, and could provide a much better environment for the girls than I could. Granted, I've had bouts of sobriety, when I felt entitled to just be able to walk back into their lives, but it has been three years, and I am just now stable enough for a hope in court. It's just going to be a lot of work, due to the fact that this new mother in my girl's life (Who I was originally thankful for) has twisted events in my children's lives she was not even present for. I realize now, that the one thing I hated about my childhood, I turned right into. It has taken me until now to realize that there are many forms of child abuse, it's not limited to two or three kinds. It's not all black and white, there is a whole grey area? I don't know if my children will ever be able to forgive me for what I have put them through (I will get further into detail in my next book). The more counseling, I receive, the more my eyes are open to this.

I remember peeking in on my oldest daughter putting her baby sissy down for a nap. "I'm not tired Sissy!" My oldest baby would yell to her little sissy. "I know you aren't." she would say as she ran her fingers through her baby sissy's hair and kissed her forehead. Those are the moments that keep me going when I feel I've fallen back to zero. As my girls napped, I popped open my bottle of cognac, sat outside with the sun on my face, and began to question how a "Loser" like me could be blessed with such good little girls. I hope after reading my story, you come out of this with an open mind. Every choice we make, creates a ripple in the water of our lives. Life is a series of cause and effect, every choice we make determines our future. I feel however, that our destiny is not set in stone, our futures ARE forever changing, and for the first time in years, I feel like I just MAY have one. I reflect on my parent's traumatic story and envy them for overcoming their problems. They are sober, happy, and have found "God" (I say, whatever works) My dad dotes over my mother, and though they have problems, as do we all, they have learned to turn to their higher power instead of that "demon bottle." I can't say in good faith that I could've taken as many blows as the both of them and survived. My parents have beaten the odds, Dad doesn't hit Mom anymore, they have a cozy little home in Michigan, and my Mother is recovering from brain surgery. We are all healing as a family, we have good days, and bad days, the point is however being that we have days period.......

Epilogue

Book II: "The Monster I've Become"

Uh, oh, Spaghetti O's....

Niccolo Machiavelli wrote, "If an injury has to be done to a man it should be so severe that his vengeance need not be feared."

We rushed back into the house. "What the hell just happened?" he said to me. An inflated sense of self entitlement filled my mind. "That bitch got what he deserved" I said, as I reflected on the events that had just taken place. We toasted our glasses with blood on our hands. While he went to change his clothes, I shot down my whiskey, and went out to the car to grab my cellphone. A chill instantly ran up my spine as I glanced down the street to my right. The police had blocked off the street, I glanced to my left, the same on that side as well.

"Here we go!" I said to myself. I returned inside grabbed my bottle and took a guzzle and lit my cigarette. "Our friends are here!" I yelled to him. I had just enough time to kick my shoes to the corner of the room, when the police plowed through the door. They immediately shot the family Pitbull, leaving behind a litter of puppies, told me to put my hands in the air. I downed my drink, and two police officers tackled me, cuffed me, and they did the same to him. On the way to the station, the officer tried to engage me in conversation. "You guys sure did a number on that poor kid, he's in the back of an ambulance as we speak!" The officer said to me. "What a bitch!" I thought to myself. He wasted no time calling the police. "Didn't his mama teach him to "Never let his mouth write a check his ass couldn't cash?" To be honest, I didn't mean for him to get hurt as bad as he did, but he stalked me! Scared me, made my life HELL! "Oh well, if he dies, I guess he dies."

"I'm not worried, I'll bail right out" I said to the officer. "I wouldn't be so smug." The officer said to me. I booked in with an attitude, and was immediately put in check when I heard my charges. Off to the pod I went. I drifted off to sleep in my cell, and this would be the last good nap I had for the next couple years of my life. I didn't realize how serious this was. I woke up to a "BAM!" I was upside down in my truck, pinned inside. "Don't move your neck ma'am! I heard. I drifted back away. I felt that Mack-truck hit me again! The lights were bright in my eyes, "back in on another heroin overdose I heard the EMT's say. What was going on? Was I in HELL? I am told Hell was all about repetition, and I had been here before. Then once again, I smelled brown sugar and my dark angel joined me...

"I woke up that morning, and something was different. There was something eerie...no air. I stumbled to the mirror, only to gasp in horror. What I saw gave me chills. Although inside, I still feel as if I am 16, the woman looking back from the mirror is a stranger to me. Something familiar is in her eyes, though her face wears the scars of a long hard life. As I look closer, this face begins to age with rapid speed. I then know who this old woman is....she's me! In the corner of the room I see her. This beautiful angel with the black cloke, she has been around my entire life. It was at that moment I realized who she was... She was "Death", and she was here to take me home....." -The Monster Inside Me

Made in the USA
Middletown, DE
30 September 2017